Up

"As someone who has struggled to keep up with Alex on a pair of New Hampshire 4,000ers in winter, I can testify firsthand to what a remarkable hiker and person she is. Patricia Ellis Herr's charming memoir distills the lessons she learned on the trail with her precocious daughter. *Up* offers a welcome corrective to Tiger Mother syndrome."

— David Roberts, author of *Finding Everett Ruess: The Life and Unsolved Disappearance of a Legendary Wilderness Explorer*

"As a parent of two kids myself, I'm always working for more quality time with cell phones and computers turned off. Some of my best times have been kayaking, hiking, and skiing with my family. It's the stuff life is built on. So I love this mother-daughter tale of sharing something beautiful and profound together and building upon those shared experiences. It's what every family should emulate. The delightful stories put a smile on my face as they brought back memories of my daughter when she was Alex's age. And it warmed my heart as they reached each summit together."

— Erik Weihenmayer, author of *Touch the Top of the World: A Blind Man's Journey to Climb Farther Than the Eye Can See* and *The Adversity Advantage: Turning Everyday Struggles into Everyday Greatness*

Up

Up

A Mother and Daughter's Peakbagging Adventure

Patricia Ellis Herr

BROADWAY PAPERBACKS
NEW YORK

BROADWAY

BROADWAY PAPERBACKS and its logo, a letter B bisected on the diagonal,
are trademarks of Random House, Inc.

Library of Congress Cataloging-in-Publication Data
Herr, Patricia Ellis.
   Up : a mother and daughter's peakbagging adventure / Patricia Ellis
Herr.
      p. cm.
   1. Mountaineering. 2. Mothers and daughters. I. Title.
      GV199.8.H47 2011
   796.522—dc23   2011034574

ISBN 978-0-307-95207-3
eISBN 978-0-307-95208-0

PRINTED IN THE UNITED STATES OF AMERICA

Photographs by Patricia Ellis Herr, except for p. 218 photograph, by
   Mark Tuckerman
Cover design by Jessie Sayward Bright
Cover photographs by Patricia Ellis Herr

10   9   8   7   6   5   4   3   2   1

First Edition

For my granite girls,
Alex and Sage.
You are the kindest,
strongest, and most beautiful
people I know.
Thanks for the many adventures.

CONTENTS

Contents

Contents

Up

"Are You Out of Your Mind?"

Since I frequently encountered this question when my five-year-old daughter, Alex, and I began climbing grown-up-size mountains, addressing it seems a fitting way to begin this account of our journey together on the trails.

The idea of hiking up all forty-eight of New Hampshire's tallest mountains started out as a casual, almost accidental lark. My daughter has been a boundless bundle of energy since birth, and I thought hiking a big mountain might prove an enjoyable occupation for us to try. I never anticipated how far we would go, nor did I anticipate how unusual our activity would strike others. At the time, I thought it would be a fun mother-daughter bonding experience and an opportunity to enjoy the riches of New Hampshire's glorious natural landscapes. I certainly had no lofty pretentions about finishing the entire list of mountains in a short amount

of time, nor did I foresee that the experience might teach her to follow her own path instead of listening to societal expectations.

As with any journey worth its salt, I came away from the trail not only treasuring the moments, the sweat, and the occasional miracle, but also taking with me some important lessons. For my daughter, I hope this experience will leave an indelible mark in her young heart, forever there to remind her that small doesn't necessarily mean weak, that girls can be strong, and that big, bold things are possible.

It was Alex who asked me to write this book. She hopes that by sharing our stories, others will experience the exhilaration of the trail. I hope the book serves as a reminder not just to Alex as she grows, but to all of us, that if you want to do something big, something daring and grand and huge, then don't automatically shrug and assume that you're too young, too old, too weak, too busy, too poor, too frazzled, or too small. Learn, persevere, sweat. Take the time to figure out how to do it correctly, then go to it with a giant spirit of adventure and enjoy the climb.

—Patricia Ellis Herr, July 2011

Some Things Will Always Be Beyond Your Control

Freak Thunderstorm on Mount Tom, August 16, 2008

Mama!" Five-year-old Alex screams to be heard over the furious storm as we crouch among the scrub near the summit of 4,003-foot Mount Tom. My ears are full of the howling wind, so though Alex crouches immediately to my right, I can barely make out her words. Even her face is obscured by the weather. The ends of her shoulder-length blonde hair fly onto her pale cheeks and into her eyes and mouth; her face is covered by dancing yellow wisps. Sage, Alex's three-year-old sister and spitting image, crouches to my left and looks intently up at my face. Her wide green eyes study my expression, looking for a clue as to how frightened she should feel.

We are 3,900 feet above sea level and in the middle of New Hampshire's White Mountains. Directly across the street lies the Presidential Range, a chain of peaks that includes Mount Washington, the highest mountain in the American Northeast and home to what the Mount Washington Observatory describes as the world's worst weather. Three storm systems converge directly over this region, making the weather subject to unpredictable variation. Even during the summer, a hiker can experience dense fog, hurricane-force winds, and temperatures hovering near the freezing point.

The morning of our adventure, the forecast had called for clear morning skies and possible afternoon thunderstorms. We had set out early, thinking we'd be back at the car well before the arrival of threatening clouds. However, true to the spontaneous nature of the Whites, an electrical tempest had formed three hours before any nasty weather was supposed to show up. Later, folks at the Mount Washington Observatory informed me that this storm didn't appear on their radar system. It gave no advance warning. It literally birthed itself right over Mount Tom. Lucky us.

"Are you scared, Mama?" Alex hollers. She too is searching for information. Should she worry? How bad is this situation? Both of my children are accustomed to hearing me speak the truth, and they look to me for guidance.

Understanding that my attitude and actions will greatly influence their emotions and their immediate behavior, I force myself to look calm. As I draw in a breath to respond, the sky opens and quarter-size hail comes pouring down. Okay, we've officially reached the point of ridiculousness. Some bored god has obviously decided to make his day interesting by upending a bucket of Dangerous Storm right over our heads.

As the hail bounces off the hoods of my young daughters' raincoats and puddles at the rubber soles of their boots, I answer Alex's question with as calm a demeanor as I can muster.

"Yes, honey. I am a little scared."

My backpack sits on the ground beside me. I had taken it off as soon as the first lightning bolt appeared, seemingly out of nowhere, on an otherwise blue and beautiful morning. In the time it had taken to remove the girls' packs and get the three of us into "lightning safe" position, the storm had fully formed and had begun to beat its chest with astounding bravado.

We crouch low beside one another, the rubber soles of our boots set firmly on the ground. The girls don't touch each other, not even to lean for support, and I don't touch them. It's important not to touch anything if at all possible, and to have only that rubber underneath our feet be in contact with the ground. If lightning strikes immediately next to us, the electricity may travel through the dirt beneath our boots. If any part of us is touching that bit of temporarily charged earth without the grounding protection of rubber, then we're toast.

We keep low, but I realize we are in danger. There are no thick groves of trees to shelter us; we crouch in pathetically tiny vegetation. We need to move, and quickly. However, I need a second or two to Not Panic. My children's safety depends entirely on my ability to keep focused.

Lightning strikes close enough for the hairs on the back of my neck to rise. The three of us let out a simultaneous shriek.

Time's up. We have to get out of here. Now.

Mount Tom isn't exactly notorious for extreme weather, and my surprise at finding myself in this situation is great indeed. When one thinks of the more dangerous peaks of New Hampshire's White Mountains, one usually considers Mount Washington, Mount Adams, Mount Lafayette, and a few other similarly bare and exposed summits. Tom is one of the easier ascents, and it is often recommended for beginning long-distance hikers. Having already climbed six of the region's highest mountains, including Mount Jefferson, an extremely rugged peak two summits away from towering Mount Washington, neither Alex nor I had expected to find today's hike a challenge. Indeed, we had even convinced little Sage to come with us. I had carried her halfway up the trail, solemnly promising her a great deal of chocolate once we reached the top. This strategy had kept her happy, and the three of us had been having an enjoyable day.

Alex and I are attempting to become members of the Four Thousand Footer Club, an Appalachian Mountain Club organization that recognizes hikers who have ascended, on foot, all forty-eight of New Hampshire's highest White Mountains. Each of these mountains is at least four thousand feet tall, and the list of official peaks is known as the New Hampshire 4Ks. Climbing all the 4Ks is normally an adult endeavor; it is rare for young children to pursue such a goal. Alex's mission is to finish the forty-eight before she turns seven, which, at the rate we are going, she should be able to do with time to spare. She is an exceptionally strong and enthusiastic hiker, always looking forward to the next ascent, and constantly talking about the mountains to anyone who will listen. When we're on the trail, I often forget that she is only five years old, as her stamina and demeanor are more characteristic of a teenager than they are of a kindergartner.

Of course, taking a young child up a mountain means bringing along all sorts of precautionary items, such as clothing for ever-changing weather, a light-weight emergency shelter, plenty of food and water, and myriad other useful and potentially lifesaving odds and ends. If I am to accompany Alex on adult-size hikes, it means I must be prepared for any contingency. My back sometimes groans at the weight of my pack, but that's a small price to pay for keeping my kid safe.

Now, however, up in the tumultuous heavens of Mount Tom, I am forcefully reminded that there is no such thing as guaranteed protection. I had brought everything but the kitchen sink and had double-checked the forecast before we left. Yet here we crouch, three lovely victims of chaos theory.

More lightning. *Enough*, I think. *Gotta go.*

I tell my daughters that we have to move, that we're not safe here, and that we need to get back down the trail and into the midst of the forest. Lightning tends to hit the tallest objects, so by surrounding ourselves with myriad trees that are uniform in height and taller than me, we lessen the risk of a strike happening to or anywhere near us. Alex looks determined and ready to roll. I stand, reach for Sage, then come to a sudden and unfortunate realization—my backpack. I can't carry both Sage and my huge pack at the same time, at least not in a full-out run. I can carry them both if I'm able to take my time . . . but right now there is no time to take. Another lightning bolt hits close by and I make a split-second decision. Get the kids out of here, secure them down below, then come back up for the pack. In the moment, that plan makes perfect sense.

"Go ahead, Alex—run, and stop at the place where we had lunch," I shout to my oldest, then swoop up Sage and run like hell.

In one second, Alex is around the corner and out of sight. We've only a couple of tenths of a mile to cover before dropping down into a heavily wooded area with tall, protective trees, and I assume Alex is just ahead of me as I dash down the trail. Sage bounces in my arms as my feet hit the slippery rocks in rapid succession. Her arms cling around my neck as I press her body close to me.

Within minutes, we reach the trail sign marking the intersection where Alex was supposed to stop. A wave of panic washes over me. Alex is not there.

There are three paths leading away from this junction, not including the path I'm standing on.

I've no idea which way my daughter went.

"Lightning position!" I bark the order to Sage as I quickly put her down. She obeys and crouches low.

"Alex!" I yell as loudly as I can, but the wind is whipping, the thunder is booming, and the hail is bouncing off the rocks. There is no way she can hear me, even if she's close by.

Sage is crying, saying something I can't understand. I kiss the top of her head, then reach into the outer mesh of her backpack to retrieve one of the many emergency whistles I require each daughter to carry.

Alex's safety now depends on this one small piece of orange plastic. Standing tall, I blow that whistle over and over and over again. The high-pitched blasts are loud enough to rival the storm's fury, and my ears ring painfully. Sage covers her head with her hands, though I'm not sure if the gesture is in protest to the piercing sound or in despair at her sister's absence.

I blow that whistle with all my heart and soul, sending out a message to my beautiful, strong child who is running the wrong way through the White Mountain wilderness.

Come back, Alex. Come back.

It is, by far, the most frightening moment of my life. Yet stubborn anger rises up and matches the fear. She cannot get lost. I won't allow it. She was only a couple of seconds ahead of me; it's impossible that she's that far ahead. She must hear this whistle, stop, and turn around. It's what I've always told both my girls to do in the event we become separated. Damn it—she'd better do it now.

The minutes drag by and still she does not appear. I think of my pack, sitting by itself on our abandoned spot of trail. My pack, which contains, among other things, a personal locator beacon. That device has a button that, when pressed, sends my direct location and personal information to search and rescue teams across the country. If I had that in my hand, I could press it, and though help would not arrive for hours (it takes time for the volunteer crews to assemble and reach the trailhead), at least people would be on their way. Should I run up and get that pack? That would mean putting Sage back into a dangerous situation. The storm still sits on this mountain, and the lightning continues to flash around us. The pack is in a dangerously exposed place. Can I leave Sage here and run after the pack by myself? No. She's three years old, and she can't be expected to hold it together and wait here alone. She'd be terrified, she might panic and run off into the woods. Then I'd end up with two missing kids instead of one.

I blow the whistle repeatedly as I pray for some definite solution to this horrible dilemma. Then, suddenly, a figure pops up on the path to my right. It is Alex, my precious child, and she is covered with mud. We run to each other, and I grab her and lift her up and kiss her dirty face.

The three of us crouch together, and Alex explains that she never saw the sign at the trail intersection, that she just ran and ran and ran. After one particularly loud thunderclap, she had crouched low and stayed put. It was then that she heard the sound of the emergency whistle. She had not immediately returned because the many flashes of lightning made her wary of standing. When she had finally started to rise, she slipped in the mud and fell over, face-first.

Alex's voice does not shake as she tells me this. She appears neither frightened nor upset. Then she tells me that she would have eventually stopped running and blown her own whistle, thus enabling me to find her. My relief at this news is massive. I try to prepare my kids for anything and everything, but of course one never knows if a child will carry out the rehearsed lesson should pandemonium actually strike.

Though we are much safer now, under the cover of many uniformly tall trees, we are still only half a mile from the summit. Lightning and thunder continue to crash about us—this storm is obnoxiously slow to move on. I would feel much better about our safety if we kept hiking downward. However, there's one not-so-little problem.

My backpack.

My backpack containing all our clothing, our food, our water, and, more important, my emergency gear, now sits all by itself in a puddle of hailstones a little way up the trail. I don't want to leave it. We've two and a half miles of slippery rock to descend before we're back at the car. If I should slip and break an ankle without my pack, then I don't have the things I need to keep all three of us warm and dry until a rescue team arrives.

I figure I can get to it in two minutes, tops, if I move as fast as I can. However, retrieving it means leaving the shelter of the taller trees and running headlong back into the lightning.

The kids have to stay here.

I place Alex immediately next to Sage and explain my dilemma. I tell my daughters that I must get that pack, that I don't feel safe hiking down without it. I tell them that I don't feel right taking them back up the trail and into the lightning we just ran from. I ask for them to understand if I run up and get the pack by myself, and I inform them that they are both safer here together, in the trees.

"How long will you be gone?" Alex asks apprehensively. It's the first tremor of fear I've detected since this calamitous adventure began.

"Not long. Five minutes at the very most."

Sage asks me not to leave. The fear leaves Alex's expression as she looks at her little sister, crouching obediently in the dirt. Then her chest puffs up and pride replaces apprehension. "Don't worry, I'll take care of you," she declares in a loud, steady voice.

"Both of you take care of each other," I respond. "I will not be gone for more than a few minutes, but to you it will probably seem like an hour. If either one of you starts to feel scared, just blow a whistle and wait. I will come to you, though it may take a few moments. Don't move from that spot, not for any reason. Remember, if you become frightened, just blow the whistles and wait."

I make them both repeat the phrase, over and over. Blow the whistles and wait. Blow the whistles and wait. It will serve as their mantra during my absence.

After kissing them both on the tops of their heads, I turn and run full speed back up the summit cone of Mount Tom.

I fly, leaping over wet rocks and roots, thinking of my huddled, frightened children crouching down among the trees. Well, actually, it's Sage I'm worried about. For whatever reason, I don't worry about Alex. She may feel frightened, but I know she will not move. We have hiked other mountains together and are used to moving as a team. There is no doubt in my mind that she will do exactly as I have instructed. Sage, on the other hand, is only three years old and inexperienced at being out in the woods. Can Alex keep her from running away if lightning strikes too close for comfort?

My feet slap in the mud and crunch over the hailstones. Where is the backpack? We didn't come up this far, did we? The trees get shorter and shorter, but still I don't see the damn thing.

Finally, a long minute or so after leaving my kids, I see a flash of orange ahead, just off the trail. It's my pack, sitting in the mud, looking forlorn, surrounded by a ring of hailstones two inches deep. I grab the pack, pull the straps over my shoulders, then turn and sprint back to my waiting children. Reaching the intersection, I yell my greetings, and both girls fly into my arms.

"Sage was about to blow her whistle because we thought you were lost!" Alex shouts, her words running together in an excited rush.

I look into Sage's eyes, which are red and teary, and I ask if she's all right.

"Yeah," her small voice murmurs. Then she squeakily declares, "You were gone a really long time!"

"Yeah!" Alex agrees.

I start to praise them for their bravery, but another close streak of lightning puts an end to the joyous reunion. The three of us join hands and scurry down the mountain. As we flee, part of me realizes that should lightning strike one of us, the electricity will flow through the other two, and all three of us will end up in serious trouble. My desire to get off the mountain pushes me onward, however, and I justify the hand-holding by telling myself that the odds of being struck by lightning while under cover of the woods are much less than the odds of one of us slipping on wet rock and breaking a limb. We therefore descend joined together, my firm grip preventing my children from taking dangerous tumbles.

We are halfway to the car when the storm finally decides to move on. The lightning fades, and its accompanying thunder goes with it, until both flash and boom disappear completely. The danger now over, I sit the girls down and give each of us a chance to catch our breath. We rest on a few rocks by a little stream and stare at one another for a while. Eventually I take a deep breath and say, "I am very proud of you both. This was a hard day, and you must have been very frightened. It just goes to show that sometimes things happen that you can't prepare for. We brought all the right stuff and checked the forecast before we left, but look what happened anyway."

Sage loses her composure and bursts into sobs. Huge tears drip down her face and fall onto the quickly disappearing hailstones. My poor kid! She must be traumatized.

Alex takes her sister's hand in an effort to comfort her, and a flurry of words spill out of Sage's mouth. I can't understand what she's saying at first, but I assume it's something about lightning or being alone or being horrifically terrified.

After patiently listening to a steady stream of weepy babble, I am finally able to extract a single word from her frenetic speech. She's been repeating it throughout her tearful tirade.

"Chocolate?" I interrupt. "Is that what you said, honey? Chocolate?"

Sage immediately ceases talking. There are a few seconds of silence, then she takes a deep breath and piteously hollers, "We didn't get to eat our chocolate!" before bursting into a fresh round of tears.

I stare confusedly at her for a moment before I realize what she's talking about. I had promised both girls a bar of chocolate when we reached the top of Mount Tom. We never reached the top, having been thwarted by the storm, so now Sage believes she's been atmospherically cheated out of her Hershey's bar.

"Oh, honey," I assure her gently, "you'll get your chocolate."

Sage stops crying and turns her little tear-stained face up toward my own. "But we didn't get to the top," she says.

"That's okay, sweetheart. You were very, very brave today. Any hiker who suffers through a thunderstorm gets a bar of chocolate, even if she doesn't actually reach the summit."

My littlest girl's face immediately brightens, and

her mouth opens in a huge, toothy smile. "Let's eat the chocolate in the car," she joyously exclaims as she lets go of Alex's hand. The next second finds her up and happily skipping down the trail.

Alex and I grin at each other, then hurry after her.

Know What You're Getting Into

Failed Mount Tecumseh Attempt, April 13, 2008

It's best to start a hiking narrative with examples of things that can go wrong, especially when your hiking partner is a very young child. My intent is not to leave readers shaking their heads with dismay, but to inform and perhaps better prepare the would-be outdoor adventurer, especially a potential parent-child team. I'm not embarrassed about the thunderstorm incident, since, in retrospect, I do believe that anyone could have found themselves in the same situation. We didn't hike into something predicted—that sucker formed right over our heads. However, the following includes an account of something that could have—*should* have—been prevented. For the benefit of those who might be spared a similar experience, I include it below.

We first stumble upon the idea by accident. The girls are running around a bench by a roadside kiosk off the Kancamagus Highway near the town of Lincoln, New Hampshire, just a few weeks after we buy our small weekend home in the White Mountains. I had just pulled over during a leisurely drive on this famous mountain road to better enjoy the views and to take advantage of the fresh air. It's March, and the snow still blankets higher ground; we can see the sun glinting off the icy peaks in the distance.

The White Mountain region is beautiful, a brilliant contrast to the drab city life we live Monday through Thursday, two hours south in Somerville, Massachusetts. I am so happy I persuaded my husband, Hugh, to buy a tiny weekend home here, for I want the girls to have a huge and regular dose of nature, and, since we intend to homeschool, an opportunity to use the natural resources around us as learning tools. Additionally, the girls need a place where they can safely run free, a place devoid of pollution, a place where there are plenty of waterfalls, trees, and hiking trails. The New Hampshire house will be our home three days a week. Even when my husband, a professor at the Massachusetts Institute of Technology, has to stay in Massachusetts because of his work, which is often, the girls and I will come here each Friday through Sunday.

Alex has been a high-energy kid since birth, always into everything and completely uninterested in remaining still. Our Somerville backyard, approximately the size of a postage stamp, does nothing to alleviate her need to move-move-move. The city playgrounds are small and filled with cold, plastic structures. The only times Alex ever seems truly happy living in Somerville are when we leave it to visit outdoor places such as Walden Pond or Drumlin Farm, both near the historic town of Concord. These two settings afford trails on which to run back and forth, sometimes giving the illusion that we are in the midst of a wide expanse of wilderness. We thought of moving to Concord, but we couldn't afford it as a one-income family.

Sage is easier to please; she's content wherever she happens to be. However, she too is happier when surrounded by trees and dirt. These places of nature breathe joy into my children; they give both my girls a peace of mind no city atmosphere can provide.

I can relate to their sentiments, for I have fond memories of roaming the outdoors as a young child. The suburbs of Columbia, Maryland, were, in the 1970s, an extremely safe community where everyone in the neighborhood knew who you were and where you lived. Most of my after-school hours were spent exploring the local creeks and playing with garter snakes. I'd come home just in time for dinner, covered in dirt and mud, feeling happy and free.

Hugh's childhood was also spent exploring the natural world. He grew up on a hundred-acre farm near Lancaster, Pennsylvania, and doesn't remember wearing shoes until the age of six. His afternoons were spent running through cornfields and climbing trees, his summers in various national parks. By the age of eleven, he was allowed to travel the country with his brothers by Greyhound bus and explore at will.

When we grew up, nature was a part of who we were and how we lived, so keeping Alex and Sage in the city day after day, month after month, has never felt right to either of us.

I watch as my daughters cavort outside the kiosk. They take turns chasing each other on the grass, faces bright with delight, cheeks red from the chill air, straight streaks of yellow hair flying every which way as they continually run, turn, and move with each other. They are the essence of Youth, and since there is no one around to disturb, I let them chase and tumble and pounce, two kittens joyfully pushing their physical and sisterly boundaries in the bright New Hampshire sunshine.

I am much less active, choosing proper, adult repose over the impromptu scamperings of childhood. My elbows lean against the kiosk's wooden rails; my forearms rest against a centered information placard. Eventually my gaze turns from my children to the content below. There's a word down there staring up at me, shouting in large bold print: Peakbaggers. Intrigued, I straighten and turn my attention to the entire text.

The short paragraphs describe a game of sorts, one in which a person ascends, on foot, a set of listed mountains. New Hampshire's local peakbagging game has an organization dedicated to the recognition of its members: the Four Thousand Footer Club. Sponsored by the Appalachian Mountain Club, it awards a certificate and a patch to those who ascend all forty-eight of the White Mountains whose summits rise above four thousand feet. I contemplate the words and think about my oldest daughter. Always a constant bundle of energy, the kid never seems to tire.

"Hey, Alex," I call out to my five-year-old, who is now running around and around the kiosk, lapping her three-year-old sister every few seconds.

"What?" she calls out breathlessly, joyously.

"Do you want to try to hike a grown-up mountain?"

Alex brings herself to a halt and looks up.

"You don't have to if you don't want to," I quickly add.

"Sure!" Her face breaks into a grin. "I want to!"

Sage runs up to my leg and asks if she can try as well. Though I strongly suspect my youngest daughter is not yet ready to hike multiple miles on her own two feet, I figure I'll give her the courtesy of allowing her to try. After all, one of the reasons Hugh and I decided to homeschool is because we feel children should be met where they're at, intellectually and otherwise. We don't want to force our children to conform to any group mean. There's no reason to instantly dismiss their goals solely because of their ages; to underestimate a child is to disrespect her. Just because Sage is three does not mean she should not be allowed to give the mountain her all. "Sure," I answer.

Both girls whoop in joyful anticipation, then resume running around and around the kiosk.

April comes a few weeks later, and, since the snow around our house has fully melted, I figure it's time to give one of these mountains a go. Mount Tecumseh, a ski mountain my family has noticed while driving into nearby Waterville Valley, is not too far from our house. A quick Google search tells me it stands more than 4,000 feet high—4,003 feet, to be exact. Another quick search reveals that its peak can be reached after only 2.2 miles of hiking—2.2 miles! Alex can do that; I'm sure of it. She hiked 4 to 6 miles every day without complaint during last year's trip to Maine's Acadia National Park, when she was only four years old. She shouldn't have any problems. Sage? Well, we'll see. We can always turn back if she gets too tired.

Though there's no snow on the ground by our house, I figure there might still be some left on the peaks, so I bundle up both excited kids in their regular snowsuits and boots. Feeling proud of myself for thinking ahead, I pack some gloves, hats, water, and food into a small backpack. How proud we'll all be when we reach the top! What a great feat we are going to accomplish! The three of us climb into our car and take off, envisioning the grand views that await us at the top of our first Four Thousand Footer.

Alex chatters nonstop all the way there, asking if we'll see any bears, if we'll need a rock climbing harness, if we'll be back in time for dinner. I answer, "No, no, and yes." I'm fairly certain our noise will keep away any bears, I know this is a hiking trail and not a climbing route, and the hour is early . . . just before noon. We should be fine.

Sage is quiet and looks out the window, and I wonder how far up the mountain she'll hike before asking to be carried. I've no expectations that she'll make it up on her own two feet, as there probably isn't enough chocolate in the world to keep her motivated all 4.4 round-trip miles. Still . . . if I carry her when she tires, the three of us should be able to summit. Sage won't be able to apply this hike toward the Four Thousand Footer Club, but since she doesn't really understand or care about this, it doesn't matter. It's Alex who appreciates the club's concept. It's Alex who possesses the strength and energy to pull this off. We'll just take it easy and see what happens.

We pull into the ski parking lot and find the "trailhead," the sign that marks the beginning of the hiking path. Mount Tecumseh Trail, the capital letters announce. I zip up the girls' coats and strap on my little backpack before leading my daughters confidently, arrogantly, into the forest.

Immediately there is a small stream crossing. We

tromp through the water and our boots do their job. Everyone's feet remain dry.

Now the path goes slightly uphill and meanders by a brook—it's beautiful. Alex comments on the sound of the falling water. "It's like music," she says. Sage is less enthralled. "Can I have a snack?" she asks.

Even though it's only been ten minutes since we left the car, I pull out a bag of trail mix and hand it to Sage, whose face brightens into a smile. Maybe that will keep her happily occupied for a good half mile or so.

We follow the stream uphill for a few hundred yards, and then we reach snow. It doesn't look like anything we can't handle. In fact, it looks inviting. The snow on the trail has been so packed down from previous hikers that it resembles a flat sidewalk. Fantastic! If it's like this all the way up the mountain, then we should be good to go.

The girls and I step onto the snow, slide a little, then find our balance and gingerly continue on our way. Sage loses a few brightly colored chocolate pieces here and there, leaving a candy zigzag behind us. We leave her consumable litter where it is for the time being, figuring that we'll pick it up on the way out.

We cross another stream, and the grade steepens, making the snow difficult to walk on. The treads of our boots don't adequately grip the surface, and the girls slip continually, sometimes catching themselves before falling into the snow, but oftentimes not. Sage begins to complain, and Alex loses her smile. Looking up, I see a relatively flat stretch just ahead and urge the girls onward.

We reach the flat stretch, but instead of experiencing a reprieve, the snow on this stretch has lost its firmness and we are no longer walking on a flat sidewalk. Every five steps, someone's foot punches through and makes a hole several inches deep. Sage continues to complain, her voice getting louder by the minute. Alex's forehead now has a furrow, and she asks if we can stop for a water break.

It's difficult to find a place to rest, since sitting means sinking into the snow. After a few minutes, we find a large rock whose flat surface is just above the snowline. I sit both girls down, dig out the water bottle, and hand it to my eldest.

Alex looks discouraged as she tilts the bottle to her lips. She doesn't seem fatigued, though. I wonder how far we've come . . . a mile? It's obvious just by looking around that we are nowhere near the summit. Can she make it all the way up? Does she want to?

Sage doesn't look discouraged. She looks downright upset.

"Are you okay, honey?" I ask.

"No," she mumbles, looking down at her lap.

"Getting tired?"

"Yes."

"Would you like me to carry you?"

"Yes."

We continue onward, Alex and I sinking inches

into the snow with every step. Sage rides on my hip, her short legs gripping my waist as I struggle not to fall over.

Fifteen minutes later, the snow suddenly gets much deeper, and it becomes almost impossible to walk. Each step gives way under our feet, and I sink up to my knees, Alex up to her thighs. I can't continue holding on to Sage, so I put her down and ask her to try a few steps. She does, and immediately sinks to her waist. She is not amused, and proceeds to loudly bemoan the fact that her boots have just filled up with snow. We trudge onward, but the snow becomes deeper still. We sink repeatedly, and we exhaust ourselves by continually having to pull our legs up out of the snow. I notice that the middle part of the trail is relatively firmer, so I tell the girls to stay in the center as best they can. They try, but they repeatedly slip, fall over, and sink.

We come to a steep hill leading down to a larger water crossing. I've no idea how we can safely get down that slope continually slipping and sinking in such deep, rotting snow. I come to a halt, look down at my miserable kids, and finally admit to myself that we are not getting up this mountain. At least not today.

Alex looks down the hill and voices my thoughts, loudly and firmly.

"I don't want to keep going, Mama," Alex declares. "I want to get up the mountain, but I don't like all this snow."

Sage's face is as screwed up as a face could possibly be.

I squat down next to them, my face level with theirs. "I'm sorry, girls. I didn't know there would be all this snow. Would you like to try again when the snow is gone?"

Alex says yes. She tells me she really wants to get up there, but not today, not until she can walk normally on dry ground. She then adds that not only is continuing on a bad idea—but that she flat out won't do it. She doesn't mean to be a bad kid, but she is *not* going one step farther in this mess, thank you very much.

Sage doesn't say anything. Her face continues to resemble that of someone with a mouthful of lemons. I reach into the bag and hand her a granola bar. Her face relaxes infinitesimally.

I'm disappointed and chagrined. I hadn't foreseen that there would be so much deep snow on the trail, and that it would be so difficult to walk on. I had thought I was well prepared, with snowsuits, boots, food, and water. Heck, I even packed a flashlight, map, and compass! Yet here we were, defeated and ready to go home.

A man hiking down from the summit approaches us. He's wearing snowshoes, and his backpack, which is much larger than mine, has a rolled-up foam mat attached to its outside. He takes a good look at both my kids, and a slight wrinkle appears across his forehead. I explain that we are about to turn back, and the wrinkle quickly disappears. "Good move—the snow just gets worse the farther up you go," he exclaims before quickly snowshoeing off. I notice *he* isn't sinking in the snow. Snowshoes! Wow, I didn't realize . . .

We make our way back toward the car, the hike becoming easier as we leave the deep snow behind. I carry Sage, since her mood has left the land of Irritated and is now residing in Outright Miserable. We reach the area of spilled chocolate, and I do my best to collect the dropped pieces.

We get back to the car, and Sage scampers into her car seat, grateful to be sitting down in a warm, familiar environment. Five-year-old Alex remains standing outside the car and watches me closely as I pop the trunk and toss in my backpack. Alex has never been one to keep her thoughts to herself, and I've a feeling I'm about to get a well-deserved earful.

"Are you okay, Alex?" I ask, and brace myself for her answer.

Though my daughter does her best to be respectful, she makes it clear this was a bungled operation. Why didn't I know about the snow? Why didn't I turn us around earlier? Wasn't there some way of knowing more about the conditions of the trail before we started? Good questions, these. They pour out of my young daughter's mouth in one long, miffed run-on sentence. My five-year-old has a wonderful capacity for language. She began to read at two years of age, and by three she was speaking in long, complex sentences.

Her verbal abilities now shine in all their glory as she scolds her mother for not being more prepared.

I allow her this outburst, as she is absolutely right. It was a foolish and ill-equipped venture. I didn't know what I was doing.

When she has finished venting, I kneel down and pull her close. "I'm sorry," I say. "You are right. I will learn more about these mountains before we attempt another hike. Do you still want to try again, after the snow has melted?"

Alex backs away from me a little so that she can look directly into my face. "Yes," she says, then kisses my cheek. "But Mama, please figure it out a little better next time."

The next two months are spent doing exactly that: figuring it out. Soon after our failed Tecumseh attempt, I find a thick book displayed on the counter of a local sporting goods store: *AMC White Mountain Guide*, compiled and edited by Gene Daniell and Steven D. Smith. I pick it up and leaf through it—wow. It contains info on every trail in the region, and it comes with a bunch of maps. When I take it to the counter, the sales representative suggests I buy an additional book, also authored by Smith and a fellow named Mike Dickerman: *The 4000-Footers of the White Mountains*. I hand over my money, take both books home, and begin to read.

Now our hiking adventures truly begin. Not by getting out there just yet, but by studying the books and the various trail maps. One of the books refers to a couple of northeastern hiking websites: Views from the Top (www.viewsfromthetop.com) and Rocks on Top (www.rocksontop.com). I access both daily, reading questions and comments from experienced White Mountain hikers.

Using the information I've gathered, I start to buy appropriate gear for all three of us. I find water-resistant hiking boots for myself and both girls. I buy backpacks—tiny, school-type ones for the girls and a large, proper daypack for me. A salesperson at that aforementioned sporting goods store walks me through the types of clothing a hiker needs to have with her. Layers are key. Something quick drying right next to the skin that wicks water and sweat away from the body. Fleece to go over that wicking base layer, to keep the body warm when the mountain air chills. A windproof, waterproof outer layer to protect the body from the harsher elements.

Along with these basics, the following items are also deemed necessary for purchase: a water treatment system; a bivy shelter (a thin, lightweight waterproof and windproof bag that resembles a tiny one-person tent, useful for accidental overnights out in the wilderness); a lightweight sleeping bag; a foam sleeping pad (to keep your body off the cold ground); a first aid kit; duct tape; a compass; sunblock; bug spray; headlamps; emergency whistles; a pocketknife; waterproof matches, and a rain cover for my pack.

The girls and I wait out the last of the spring thaw by hiking flat, snow-free trails at lower elevations to try out our boots and gear. We walk for hours at a time, Alex consistently happy and strong, and Sage content as long as we don't go more than four miles. At the end of our hikes, Sage is worn out while Alex only seems energized. There is no doubt in my mind that if we attempt a snow-free Tecumseh, Alex will summit. I read and reread the two guidebooks while the three of us wait for the springtime sun to dry out the trails.

"I Think I Can" Works

Peak #1: Mount Tecumseh, June 7, 2008

The first day of June arrives, and the Internet forums are flooded with descriptions of snow-free
mountains. Alex and I are eager to reattempt Mount
Tecumseh. Sage says she also wants to try again, but I
strongly suspect her enthusiasm is counterfeit. While
Alex is genuinely interested, Sage is eager to please.
The difference between the two types of motivation is
huge and easy to mark. In spite of my doubts about
Sage, I allow her to participate in picking the date of
what we jokingly refer to as "Tecumseh, Take Two."
Both girls want to go as soon as possible, so we choose
the upcoming Saturday, June 7. Later that evening,
after the girls are tucked into bed and safely out of earshot, I ask my husband, Hugh, to accompany us on this
hike so that Sage won't feel any pressure to continue
should she tire. If she decides at any point that she's
had enough, then Hugh can take her back down the

mountain while Alex and I ascend. He agrees, and I go to bed relieved. I don't want Sage put in a position where she feels pressured to keep going when her body is too tired to continue. I also don't want to have to turn back if all is going well for Alex. Each child should be given the opportunity to hike as much or as little as she can.

The four of us arrive at the ski parking lot bright and early on June 7, just half an hour after finishing breakfast. This time around, I carry a much larger pack filled with wicking layers, fleece, rain gear, plenty of food, water, a water filtering system, a first aid kit, a map, a compass, headlamps, sunblock, bug spray, the bivy shelter and foam sleeping mat, and a Swiss Army knife. We are clad in shorts and short-sleeve shirts made from synthetic fibers, and our feet are protected with waterproof hiking boots. The morning air is warm, but not muggy, and the bugs are not yet out. Our spirits high, we step off the road and into the woods.

The water crossing by the trailhead is just a trickle of water today, nothing like the ankle-deep stream we encountered a couple of months ago. We step over it easily, not even wetting the soles of our boots. Up the small hill and alongside the brook we amble, admiring the sounds of the splashing water and commenting on the merits of dry, dirt trail. Our hike is so much simpler without all the snow. There's no slipping or sliding, no sinking, no snow-filled boots.

We cross another brook, this one wider and deeper than the one at the beginning of the trail. Alex hops from rock to rock with a giant grin on her face. Sage slowly steps across, looking nervous but determined.

There's another hill to tackle, this one longer and steeper. It must have been here a couple of months ago, but everything looks completely different without all the snow, and I don't remember this part of the trail. Luckily, many of the trees along the trail are "blazed," marked with a yellow rectangle at adult eye level, so at no time do we feel unsure of which way to go.

Alex climbs up with her head held high and her eyes taking in every bit of the wooded landscape. Sage putters along in a shuffling fashion, so I take her hand and sing silly songs to lighten her mood. She responds by smiling, but her brow is wrinkled and she doesn't look happy. We're only a half mile into the hike, but I've no doubt my three-year-old will not make it to the top unassisted. This doesn't bother me, for I never expected her to climb something of this magnitude; she is, after all, only three years old. I give silent thanks for Hugh's willingness to join us today; his assistance will most likely be needed.

The trail flattens out, and Sage's mood slightly improves. Alex continues to act as though we're just taking a casual stroll down our Somerville street.

A few minutes later, we reach our previous point

of return. The trail now turns steeply downward and crosses fast-moving Tecumseh Brook. Luckily, there are large boulders on which to step, and the brook at this point is narrow. We cross without difficulty, then stop to rest by the loud, splashing water. I hand each girl a bottle of juice and some trail mix. Alex looks good. She doesn't seem tired, and she hasn't yet uttered one word of complaint. Sage, however, shows signs of extreme fatigue, and her countenance is less than cheerful. According to our guidebook, we have hiked 1.1 miles. There's still more than a mile to go before we reach the summit. Then, of course, we'll have to hike all the way back down.

Ten minutes of drinking and eating later, we resume our hike and begin climbing steeply away from the brook. Halfway up this bit of trail, Sage throws in the towel and asks to be carried. Hugh promptly complies. Alex continues to hike strongly, asking only for a drink every now and then.

Fifteen minutes and much huffing and puffing later, we reach a viewpoint where a very short side path diverges and leads to a ski slope. Hugh needs to sit down for a while; he's in pain and isn't sure he can carry Sage much longer. Hugh is a rock climber, a runner, and a hiker, but his legs are artificial. Every once in a while, and in no predictable fashion, his stumps chafe painfully against his prosthetic sockets, and walking becomes an agonizing chore. Though he had started the hike in good form, his stumps are now causing him much grief. I offer to give him the backpack so I can take Sage, but he explains that the trade won't make much of a difference. I ask if he wants to turn back, but he tells me no, not yet.

We sit, eat trail mix, and discuss our options. Sage declares that she's no longer having any fun, even though she hasn't walked at all since the last water crossing. I ask Alex how she's doing. She says that she's tired, but that she feels good and wants to keep going. Her can-do attitude is temporarily infectious, for Sage immediately declares that she wants to keep trying too. Again, I note the difference between my two girls. Alex means what she says; she is genuinely interested in ascending. Sage, however, is just mimicking her sister, wanting to copy whatever her personal heroine says and does. My husband and I look at each other uneasily but agree that we'll keep at it. After ten minutes, we pick ourselves up and continue the ascent.

The trail immediately becomes incredibly steep and a million times rockier. Our feet must constantly step up and over large chunks of stone. We creep along, our pace slowing to that of a dying snail. Alex slows down, but remains determined and happy. Sage, in spite of the fact that she is being carried, starts to grumble. I hand her some trail mix, and she is temporarily placated.

We reach the top of one steep stretch, turn a slight

corner, and are immediately confronted with another long and steep stretch. I ask Hugh how he's doing. He says he's fine, but I suspect he's not telling the truth. Sage takes one look up at the trail ahead of us and announces she does not want to continue. Alex gives her a surprised and angry look. "You're not even hiking!" she exclaims.

"Hugh, what do you want to do?" I ask. He grits his teeth and grunts, "I can still go on for a bit." He continues upward, Sage held tightly in his arms. The mother in me wants to tell him to turn around right now and take care of his stumps. The wife in me knows it's best to let him make his own decisions; Hugh does not like being told what to do, by anyone. I try to make Sage smile by singing another silly song. She glowers me into silence.

At the end of the second steep stretch, we turn the corner to find . . . yet another steep stretch. I had read that this second mile would be one long never-ending steep section, but reading the words did not adequately prepare me for the reality. I had thought there might be at least *some* flat bits between the vertical parts. Unfortunately, the grade never eases, and every time we turn a corner, we're greeted with the same onerous sight: a long, rocky, incredibly steep path leading up, up, up.

My legs hurt, and I'm getting annoyed with this trail. To make matters worse, the June blackflies awake and emerge from the woods around us. These nuisances take no notice of our slathered-on bug repellent and head straight for our eyes and mouths. We're forced to wave our arms in a futile measure of self-defense as we drag ourselves onward, the sweat dripping off our faces as the sun climbs higher in the late morning sky.

Sage sucks a bug into her mouth by accident, and that does it. The poor kid has now had quite enough. "It's a howwible, howwible day," she wails after she inadvertently swallows the little critter. We stop, my husband puts Sage down, and the four of us discuss the situation.

Sage wants to go back. Hugh's stumps are probably bleeding by now. Alex asks if we can keep going, even as she flicks a bug off her arm. "No!" Sage shouts in despair. The time has obviously come to put our plan into action. Actually, we probably should have put it into action half a mile ago. Hugh asks Sage if she would like to sit with him for a while and then turn back while Alex and I continue. She nods her head so vigorously that I fear she'll slip a cervical disc. I give Hugh one of the water bottles and some extra food; then I kneel and hug Sage. I tell her I am very, very proud of her. She glares at me. Alex and I bid Hugh and Sage adieu, then we continue our ascent.

Once alone, I ask Alex how she's doing. "Fine," she answers. She *is* doing fine, very fine indeed. Now that it's just the two of us, we hike markedly faster than before; though my five-year-old daughter is no doubt tired, her natural pace is twice that what it was with her little sister in tow.

There are a few more steep sections left, then the trail finally levels out for good. I suggest that we sit and chug some water. Alex heartily agrees.

"How are you doing?" I ask. "Still fine," Alex answers. Her hand swats away one of the many flies that have followed us up the trail. "Want to turn back?" I ask, knowing full well Alex will not want to do such a thing, especially not after conquering all those nasty steep bits. "No," she answers with a smile. "We're almost at the top—I'm not stopping now!"

We sit for a few minutes and savor the moment. We're about to summit our first 4K, and we both realize that this will mark the beginning of something wonderful. Alex will forever know that she can climb mountains of this magnitude, and fairly easily at that. I will forever know that I gave my kids a shot at something huge. I took them both seriously and allowed them to do their best. I'm proud of them both, especially Sage. Sage did what she could; she truly gave it her all. For that, she has my utmost respect.

Of course, on this particular day, just before reaching this particular summit, I've no idea just how monumental this occasion will actually be. I don't know that June 7, 2008, will mark the beginning of Alex's fifteen-month peakbagging spree. I don't realize how dedicated Alex will soon become to this quest, or that she'll end up summiting all forty-eight Four Thousand Footers before losing her first baby tooth. All I know in that moment is that we're almost at the top of Mount Tecumseh, that we're both hot and sweaty, and that we're both grinning like maniacs.

"Are you ready?" I ask. Alex nods. We get up, walk a few minutes over some blessedly flat land, climb another steep, but blessedly short, section—and we're there!

A small pile of rocks, serving as a cairn, sits on a flat boulder and marks the official high point. Alex runs to it, whooping with pride and joy. Smacking her five-year-old hand on the topmost stone, she hollers, "I did it!" Happiness pours out of her skin, and her face beams with pride. She stands, victorious. I walk up to her, touch the cairn, kneel, and give her a giant hug.

"I knew you could do it, Alex," I tell her.

"How did you know?" she asks, the corners of her smile almost reaching her ears.

"I knew because *you* knew. *You* knew you could, so *I* knew you could." I congratulate her on her first 4K, then take out my disposable camera to mark the occasion.

There isn't much of a view from this summit, as the cairn is almost completely surrounded by trees. If we stand and peer through a gap in some branches, we are able to see a partial view of the valley below. This little bit of vista is enough to sufficiently impress Alex, and she declares the scene "so beautiful!" After a few minutes of standing and peering, we sit and share a chocolate bar.

"What about Sage?" Alex asks, after her part of the chocolate has been keenly devoured.

"What *about* Sage?"

"You said you knew I could do it. What about Sage? Did you know she couldn't?"

I smile at my daughter, so incredibly astute.

"Sage is very young, Alex, and her legs are shorter than yours. Also, she didn't really want to do this today."

"She said she did."

"Only because she knew you and I wanted to."

Alex is silent for a moment, then takes out various writing utensils and paper from her backpack. She sketches a picture of the mountain. It looks like a giant, upside-down V. As she draws a narrow, green-topped tree at the very top of the sharp peak, she asks, "It's okay that Sage didn't want to, isn't it?"

"Of course!" I answer. "In the future, she'll probably stay home with Papa . . . and that's fine. I don't want her to feel like she has to hike in order to please you and me."

Alex finishes the first tree and goes to work on a second, wider one, situated at a precarious angle, just below the summit. I watch as she shades in the

houselike trunk, then creates a mass of similar-looking figures up and down both sides of her impossibly sloped mountain. She asks how to spell "Tecumseh." I tell her, and she writes in big, print letters across the page.

Ignore the Naysayers

Peaks #2 and #3: Mount Eisenhower and Mount Pierce,
June 21, 2008

"Moose!" I sputter as my foot hits the brakes on my little Honda Civic, bringing it to a screeching halt along Route 302. The huge, imposing creature—obviously a male—stands halfway out of the woods, its two front hooves on the asphalt of the road's shoulder, its two back hooves in the grass under the trees. This is the first time I've ever seen a moose, and I'm awestruck. The bull reacts to my sudden stop by bounding back into the forest. It doesn't go so far as to disappear from view, however. Instead, it stands just beyond a close row of trees and keeps its massive head turned in our direction. Slowly, I drive my car onto the shoulder and come to a stop inches from where those majestic hooves so recently stood. Knowing these animals are unpredictable, I leave the car running in case we need to make a quick getaway.

"Alex!" I exclaim, trying to rouse my daughter. We

had left our house at 5:30 this morning in order to get an early start on what will potentially be our second 4K, 4,761-foot Mount Eisenhower. Though a good sport about getting out of bed before dawn, Alex had promptly fallen back to sleep soon after we had gotten on the road. She now snoozes away, securely strapped into her car seat, the top half of her body slumped over in that contorted posture only young kids can successfully attain. "Alex, moose!" I repeat.

Alex stirs, blinks a few times, then sits up dutifully and tries to focus her eyes. "Moose!" I say yet again, frantically gesticulating toward my driver's seat window.

Alex catches sight of the moose, who is still standing erect, staring at the car. "Wow!" she murmurs, shaking off her early-morning cobwebs.

"Don't get out," I instruct. "We don't want to provoke it."

We look out our window and admire the bull for a few long and glorious minutes. Its big brown eyes blink, and I wonder what it thinks about us rapturously staring human creatures. This fellow is an intriguing display of nature's handiwork. The body is massive—at least seven feet tall and six feet long—yet it's supported by four very skinny, spindly legs. The broad, handsome antlers protrude upward and outward from an impossibly narrow head. It's an interesting juxtaposition of opposites.

"This is pretty cool, yes?" I ask Alex. "Yeah!" she

answers, beaming. We stare a few minutes longer; then I slowly pull back onto the road. Ten minutes later, we arrive at the small parking lot adjacent to the Edmands Path trail.

Edmands Path, named after J. Rayner Edmands, a prominent trail builder during the late-nineteenth and early-twentieth centuries, has a reputation for being an extremely pleasant way to ascend Mount Eisenhower. The guidebooks describe its three-mile length as relatively gentle in slope with good footing. Most trails in the Whites are rocky—we are, after all, in the Granite State—but Edmands Path is reportedly less so. It seems a good choice for Alex, who has been asking to attempt another 4K ever since we climbed Mount Tecumseh two weeks ago. Mount Eisenhower will be a hike of greater distance, more than six miles round-trip, but if at any point it becomes too much for my daughter, then we'll simply sit and rest. I've no problem turning back if necessary—however, if Alex does indeed make it up there, I know her eyes will be rewarded with much more than the sight of a treed-in cairn.

Smith and Dickerman's *The 4000-Footers of the White Mountains* describes Mount Eisenhower as having a bald dome for a summit; therefore we should experience 360-degree views. The mountain's position along the Presidential Range will enable us to see Mount Washington, Mount Franklin, and Mount Pierce, not to mention many other, farther-away Four Thousand Footers. This morning's forecast contained the terms *mild, dry,* and *cloudless*—in other words, we should have a breathtakingly beautiful time of it up there.

Alex and I enjoy the first mile very much. My daughter takes typical five-year-old delight in hearing her feet *thunk-thunk* upon the various wooden planks that bridge a couple of streams. Little flowers bloom here and there, tiny and delicate and beautiful. Our conversation is chipper as Alex and I make continual comments on the greenness of the leaves, the cool feel of the morning air, and the trickling sounds of water chasing itself over rocks and pebbles. We reminisce about our morning moose, and concur that life is good. It's a grand thing, being out on a trail in the forest, ambling along, happily anticipating the views from the top of a good, solid mountain. We move slowly, luxuriously, and stop frequently to pamper our senses. Hikers pass in twos and threes, adults hiking at their normal pace, all of them happy, just like us, each of them reveling in the day's glory.

Everything is almost too good to be true. And then, suddenly, it isn't.

"How old are you, honey?" A bulky man plants himself before us and asks the question of Alex in a voice most people use when talking to infants. He's the only hiker who has passed but not continued upward with a smile. Instead, he has come up from behind, overtaken us, and then turned to purposely stop us in our tracks. Though my instincts tell me not to worry, I fully straighten my nearly six-foot self and bring a hand to the pepper spray hanging from my belt.

Alex never appreciates being spoken to with any voice that isn't also used for adults. If this man wasn't blocking the trail, she would have politely smiled and kept walking. As this is not possible, she turns her face downward and takes a step toward me.

"She's five," I answer, placing my hand on her shoulder.

Continuing to look at Alex, the man inquires, "And how far are you going?" Again, his voice is over-the-top sweet, as though he has somehow mistaken Alex for a mentally challenged puppy.

Alex neither lifts her head nor answers. I force a smile and explain that we hope to make it to the top.

For the first time since coming to a halt in front of us, the stranger looks up and meets my gaze. His angry eyes surprise me with their intensity. His glare is filled with righteous indignation, and for a moment I worry that I have accidentally offended him. Why is he so angry? I experience another second or two of bafflement, and then I get it. He isn't used to seeing young kids on mountain trails, so he's worried about Alex. He thinks I'm dragging her along, forcing her to do something that's beyond her interest and ability. The concept of a small child doing this happily and enthusiastically is foreign to him, so he assumes I'm marching her up.

The man finally breaks eye contact and turns his attention back to Alex.

"Well, aren't you sweet for trying!" Man, that voice is annoying. Alex's shoulder tenses beneath my hand. "It's a long way though—a little girl like you shouldn't be trying to hike such a big, grown-up mountain."

Oh, dear. I need to get Alex out of here before she explodes. My daughter's whole body is now stiff with outrage. I can feel the frustration and anger radiating off her, and I've no idea how long it will be before she unleashes her incensed, adult-size vocabulary on this condescending fellow. I strengthen my hold on her shoulder.

"Oh, I think we'll be all right," I answer.

"I wasn't talking to *you*," the man snaps without even looking at me. His eyes remain on Alex, who is glowering so intently at the ground that I expect little plumes of smoke to start rising from the dirt at any moment.

"Maybe your mama should take you home now." The sugar in his voice could choke an elephant. Alex starts to shake. I understand the emotional hurricane that's going on within her—she is being underestimated, something she cannot tolerate. My grip on her shoulder tightens even more as I say in a raised and unwavering voice, "Thanks for your concern, but we're really all right. Have a nice day now."

The man throws me another look of death, then finally turns his bulk around and continues up the trail.

Alex is seething. I look down at her face, and she looks as though she wants to attack something, anything. I wait until I think the man is out of earshot; then I release my daughter's shoulder and we move forward. As soon as we round the nearest bend, my forty-inch firecracker explodes.

"Why did he talk to me like that?" she roars. I don't attempt to quell her volume. The poor kid has a right to vent her fury after such a frustrating encounter.

"Why did he say we should go home? Why did he call me a little girl?" Alex marches along, slamming her feet into the ground, pushing herself forward in a full-blown, five-year-old huff.

"He thought I was making you hike up this mountain," I explain as I quicken my pace to match my daughter's flying, ferocious footsteps. "He saw you and assumed you couldn't possibly reach the top."

"Why did he think that? Was I *limping*?!"

Suppressing a smile, I reach out, grab hold of Alex's backpack, and bring her to a halt. She swivels her body around and looks up at me.

"Alex," I gently intone, "have you seen any other kids on this mountain?"

"No."

"What about Tecumseh? Did you see any other kids on that hike?" I ask.

Alex thinks for a minute, then answers, "No. I mean, except for Sage."

"Do you think you're going to see any kids today?"

"Well, . . . maybe a teenager."

"What about kids your size? Your age?"

I remain quiet to see if she'll connect the dots on her own. This strategy doesn't work, as she eventually answers my silence with an impatient "So?"

"When people see something they aren't used to seeing, they question it," I explain. "Some then accept what they see and change what they believe accordingly. Others refuse to change their minds, no matter what. Such people try to make what's in front of them fit the model they already have in their heads, even if the model is wrong."

Alex stares at me intently, trying to understand. "So," she begins slowly, "he saw me and thought that kids can't hike up mountains. Instead of seeing me and changing his mind . . . ," she trails off, trying to find the right words to express her thoughts.

"He decided to make you fit what he believes," I say. "He doesn't believe kids your age can hike up mountains; therefore he wanted you to turn around. Even though you're doing fine, even though you *can* hike up mountains. He wanted to make you fit in with his ideas about children."

Alex blinks incredulously at me for a moment, as though she can't believe her ears. "Well, *that's* stupid," she finally declares. Then she marches up the mountain ahead of me on her own two very willing and capable feet.

Our previously halcyon atmosphere has now been infiltrated by negative thoughts and emotions. That simply won't do, so I get to work restoring my child's happy state of mind. As we make our way up a straight and steep pitch, I ask Alex if she wants to sing a song. She looks dubious, but I go ahead and launch into a loud version of "Bringing Home a Baby Bumblebee." The lyrics brighten her mood, and she giggles as I sing in an obnoxious, goofy voice. Though I temporarily ruin the wilderness experience for a couple of passing hikers, I manage to bring the spark back into my child's beautiful blue eyes. When I finish, Alex cheers.

Next comes a series of word games. We make up rhymes; we take the letters of our names and list words that start with those same letters; we trade riddles. Alex's riddles are the kind that don't make much sense unless you're five years old, but the exchanges are enjoyable nevertheless.

The trees are getting shorter as we gain altitude. Alex asks if we're close to the top. I consult my ripped-out page of Smith and Dickerman's book and read the trail description. Part of me twinges as I do so, as I can hear my elementary school librarian scolding me for damaging a printed work of art. My mind tells that voice to shush—it's my book, and I'm using it as the guides intended: to retrieve information about a trail. Besides, the whole thing is too damn heavy to carry in my backpack.

I read, then conclude that we're probably about a mile from the summit, but only half a mile before we step out of the trees and venture onto open, high-altitude rock. I share this information with Alex, who nods approvingly, then asks if we can take a snack break before continuing onward.

The two of us sit side by side and munch organic energy bars. Alex looks good, and I congratulate myself on taking her mind off our aggravating and unfortunate earlier encounter. I ask her how she feels, and she replies that she's tired but looking forward to "having some good views."

Several more hikers trek by as we rest, each of them breaking into a smile when they see Alex. One small, thin lady carrying a backpack twice her size gives Alex a big thumbs-up. Alex beams at her and waves.

Eventually we put ourselves back on our feet and hike onward. We walk in happy silence, feeling well sated and eager. The trees are thinning, getting very short indeed . . . and then we step out into the sun. We've entered that magical place known as "above tree line."

Oh my. There is a gasp at my side as Alex takes in the splendor before us. I don't look down to see her expression though, not just yet. I'm too busy absorbing the view myself.

A massive peak looms to our immediate northeast, little dots of moving hikers peppering the trail that runs across its crest. *That's Mount Franklin,* my mind whispers, recalling the detail from Smith and Dickerman's guidebook. It's beautiful. So large, and yet right there . . . I feel like I can reach out and touch it.

Miles and miles of trees carpet its flank; the greenery stretches downward and westward as far as the eye can see. We can see 5,716-foot Mount Jefferson in the distance. It's a high, rocky bump to the north-northeast, silhouetted against a perfectly blue sky. The view to the east and south is blocked by the summit cone of Mount Eisenhower itself, as Edmands Path winds its way up the mountain's west and north side. Clouds float lazily above our heads, fat and slow and free.

The vision is more beautiful than I had imagined. I have traveled widely and seen many stunning landscapes. This, however—there is something about this that takes every bit of my breath away. We are up on high, in the New Hampshire heavens, and it took us only a few hours of steadfast walking to get here.

I stand in a daze, only faintly hearing Alex exclaim, "Mama, this is so beautiful!" The two of us stay there for a long while, taking it all in. Eventually I look down into my daughter's face, and what I see moves me tenfold more than the mountaintop vista. My precious daughter, whose legs are half as long as mine and who unwaveringly hiked up this giant, "grown-up" mountain, is consumed with what can only be described as pure joy. She is touched by this, and profoundly so. If she is lucky, she will remember this moment for the rest of her life. The times she is troubled, the times when she feels life is just too much, the time some jerk of a boyfriend breaks her heart, the times when life's inevitable failures threaten to break her down—I hope she looks back to this moment in her very young life and remembers that Beauty can always be found.

Love for my child overwhelms me; it threatens to flatten me. I am so lucky to have this incredible, strong, intelligent little girl in my life! It takes every ounce of willpower not to embrace her in a bear hug right that very second. I refrain from such a move, however, for I've no wish to interrupt Alex's gazing. She is forming her own moment with nature, and it would be wrong of me to intrude. I return my gaze to the mountains and leave my child to her own quiet reflections.

We eventually move on, stepping carefully along the remainder of the Edmands Path until we reach the intersection with the Mount Eisenhower Loop. I snap a picture of Alex at this junction. She smiles proudly as she holds on to the wooden trail sign. My new digital camera gives me immediate feedback: the photo is perfect, my daughter's pink shirt is nicely juxtaposed against a deep blue sky.

From here, it's a steep few tenths of a mile up the rocky summit cone. We ascend slowly, step after step after step; Alex is tiring. The trail flattens out a bit, and then, finally, we reach the huge cairn that marks Eisenhower's high point.

Alex is smiling, happy, proud. The 360-degree views are incredible: mountains sprawl before us in every direction; they cluster in giant bumps near and far on the horizon. Mount Monroe, Mount Washington, and the

northern Presidentials are there, just right over there, a handsome family of peaks posing for the perfect photograph.

We sit and eat more energy bars, Alex glowing in the pride of her accomplishment. Large and small groups of hikers walk by, each individual within them offering a hearty phrase of congratulations before continuing on his or her way. "Did you make it up here all by yourself?" "You are so strong!" "I wish I had started that young!" Each voice is genuine, each smile is wide, each greeting is cheerful. Alex's spirits rise so high that I half expect her to float off the mountaintop, a blonde balloon flying on her merry and innocent way.

We spend many minutes up there, perhaps close to sixty. Then, just as I ready myself for the return to civilization, Alex asks, "What's that mountain over there?"

She is standing and pointing at a very close peak directly to our southeast.

"Mount Pierce, I think."

"Is it a Four Thousand Footer?"

I smile and nod, approving of where this is apparently going.

"How far away is it?"

We pull out the map and look at it together. The distance from here to there is a mile and a half from summit to summit, walking along the ridge. I notice a trail down from Pierce that would deposit us on the road roughly two miles from our car.

"Can we go over there?"

"Now?" I'm unsure of Alex's endurance, and I don't want to wear her out. However, she seems extremely enthusiastic.

"Yes, now," she answers, a trace of impatience in her voice.

Part of me worries that she will tire, but a greater part of me doesn't want to stand in her way. I decide to continue.

After the climb down Eisenhower's summit cone, the hike to 4,312-foot Pierce is easy. Never gaining or losing much altitude, Alex and I move swiftly. We talk incessantly, covering a great number of subjects in a short amount of time. We discuss pirates (they must have had terrible childhoods); the pros and cons of being a rock (one never experiences death . . . but also, one never experiences life); whether Curious George was really a monkey or an ape (he certainly looks like an ape, in spite of what the book states); and a variety of other important topics. We pause in our conversation every now and then to greet other hikers. To each, Alex chirps, "Hi!" before skipping on her way. My daughter is, in a word, happy.

We reach the summit of Pierce, throw our backpacks on the ground, and sit by the cairn. The view is less astonishing than the view from Eisenhower, but it still offers lovely vistas to the north and northeast. As we relax, a pair of women give Alex chocolate, then offer to take our picture. We thank them and mug for the camera. Life is grand, and we feel fantastic.

The pleasant bearers of chocolate take their leave, and Alex and I are left to ourselves. We sit side by side, backs against the cairn, legs stretched out in front of us. We listen to the glorious silence and stare at the round dome of Eisenhower, a mile and a half away. The minutes tick lazily by. If the two of us could just stay right where we are for a few days, just like this, well, that would be marvelous.

My daughter eventually speaks.

"That man was wrong."

"What man?" I ask, my mind too busy with the immediate present to bother itself with the recent past.

"The man coming up the trail. The man who said I should turn around."

"Oh." Now I remember, though I'd rather not. "Yes, Alex. He was wrong."

Alex is silent for a few minutes. I watch wispy clouds crawl across the sky; they move almost imperceptibly.

"He said I couldn't get up Eisenhower. I did, and then I got up Pierce."

I remain silent, but turn my eyes toward Alex's face. She looks pensive, as though her mind is examining a new concept.

"So when someone tells me I can't do something—if they say it's too hard for me—I shouldn't always believe them."

"That's right," I say. "If you think you can do something, then do it. Ignore those who say that you shouldn't even try."

We eventually descend Mount Pierce, though neither one of us really wants to. I am tired on the descent, and my pace starts to drag. Alex, on the other hand, rides her second wind down the mountain. She's a bundle of energy, skipping over roots and leaping over rocks, blowing past groups of adults. I find it difficult to keep up.

One descending couple keeps passing us, then we pass them, then they pass us. We finally decide to hike out together. They're a very friendly husband and wife who have young kids of their own. After a few minutes of lovely conversation, I sheepishly ask if they'll give us a ride back to our car after we reach the road. We parked by Edmands Path to go up Mount Eisenhower, but since we descended Mount Pierce, we're two miles away from our car. The nice folks graciously agree, and Alex and I are spared the road walk.

Chattering away nonstop, Alex acts as though she's been slipped some espresso. My guess is that she is experiencing the "hiker's high," that adrenaline rush that sometimes overtakes someone at the end of a long hike. The high lasts until the moment she gets into our car, and then her giddy demeanor finally fades. Alex yawns as I start the engine, then asks if we can stop for a bagel on the way home. I answer in the affirmative, but before we are out of the parking lot, she is fast asleep.

Lose the Paranoia

Peaks #6 and #7: Mount Osceola and East Osceola, August 2, 2008

Hello!" The ax-wielding, shirtless young man congenially booms at my child. "Hi!" Alex responds, grinning widely. She doesn't seem to notice the large instrument of violence this brawny twentysomething grips in his muscular right hand.

I look up at this scene, the bottom half of my body hanging over a precipitous drop known as the chimney. We are halfway between 4,340-foot Mount Osceola and 4,156-foot East Osceola, our sixth and seventh 4Ks. My hands clutch the granite ledge as I freeze in surprise, the top half of my body leaning toward solid ground while my feet dangle in midair. I did not hear this fellow coming, caught up as I was in assisting Alex safely up this miniature rock face. My daughter hadn't actually needed much help; her small fingers had found a dozen tiny holds, and she scampered up without a moment's hesitation. Being her mother, I had fretted in spite of her agility and had followed closely beneath her quickly ascending feet. Once she was safely over the ledge, I looked down only for a moment in an attempt to find proper footholds. When I looked back up, there he was.

I stare at this smiling fellow for a second or two, my body temporarily shocked into immobility. Then, thankfully, two words flit through my startled brain: trail worker.

A trail worker. Of course. This must be one of those good people who habitually clear the trails of fallen trees and logs. Many of these hearty volunteers go off and have a nice wander about the woods once their duties are finished for the day. So this fellow is, in all probability, harmless. But still. I am horribly aware that if this person does happen to have sinister intentions, there is precious little I can do to prevent him from harming Alex. He is standing right next to her, and I am suspended over a small cliff. The trail is well populated today, and in all probability someone will come along at any moment; however, a fellow with nefarious motives needs only a few seconds.

"Hello!" I return his enthusiastic greeting in a loud voice while trying to appear relaxed and cheerful. I haul myself up, readjust my backpack straps, and walk toward my daughter. "Want some water?" I ask, reaching for the Nalgene bottle that conveniently hangs next to my reassuring canister of pepper spray. Alex takes the liquid and drinks.

"How are you doing today?" I ask in a voice that sounds anything but natural. I'm a horrible actress.

The young man's smile widens. "Oh, I'm fine, thanks! Off to explore the path less taken!" And with that, he turns and disappears into the trees, ax slung comfortably over his shoulder.

Moments later, a couple approaches, descending from Mount Osceola. My dumbfounded expression raises their eyebrows, and I ask if they have recently seen a man carrying a large ax. "Oh yes," the woman answers. "He was just at the summit, chatting us up. He's a trail worker."

Told you so, I chide myself. Why else would a guy with an ax walk around up here? The average killer doesn't hike four miles up a steep and rocky trail to look for potential victims. That's a little too much effort; it's much easier and more profitable to kidnap folks from suburban streets or attack them at highway rest stops. I grin at my foolishness.

Alex and I continue up the steep and rocky path, clambering over large chunks of boulder as we make our way back up Mount Osceola. It's our second time on this section of trail today. We had touched the summit this morning, then continued one mile to East Osceola. After reaching that mountain's viewless peak, we had turned around and headed back the way we had come, which meant retracing our steps down East Osceola and then once again ascending Mount Osceola. The trail between the two mountains is almost vertical in places, and drops of sweat roll down our faces as we push ourselves up the final few tenths of a mile. My thoughts race along with my heartbeat.

Why didn't Alex shy away from the trail worker? Shouldn't she have been a bit wary? Shouldn't she have realized that standing right next to someone she doesn't know (especially someone with an ax!) when I'm not right there to protect her is an unwise thing to do?

Maybe, maybe not. Statistically speaking, it makes sense not to worry. In the small handful of violent crimes that have occurred within the White Mountain backcountry during the last couple of decades, each victim already knew his or her assaulter. Robberies on the trail are nonexistent, unless you count the occasional black bear getting into your food at night or a local gray jay swooping down and flying off with your sandwich. The people one meets on a trail are relaxed and easygoing. Everyone is too busy enjoying the scenery to contemplate committing a felony. As a consequence, when hikers cross paths with one another, there are smiles and spoken pleasantries all around. Alex must have picked up on the absence of "stranger danger" up here.

Not that we abide by strict "stranger danger" rules, anyway. Of course, both my kids know enough not to get into a car or walk away with a stranger, and they both know to fight like mad should someone they don't know attempt to pick them up. Speaking with strangers, however, has never been expressly forbidden. Perhaps that flies in the face of conventional wisdom, but I feel it's ridiculous to tell children not to do something they see their parents do every day. We have to talk to strangers, all the time, every one of us. The grocery store clerk is a stranger, as is the person who takes our tickets at the movie theater. We ask strangers to give us the time, we ask them for directions, we even hold the doors open for them when they enter a building behind us. Is it possible to go an entire day without talking to a stranger? I seriously doubt it.

That being said, I'm out here hiking with my blonde-haired, blue-eyed, five-year-old daughter. Though the odds are astronomically against our running into someone we wouldn't want to meet, Alex must be made to understand that she can't stand right next to someone she doesn't know unless I'm standing there with her. I don't ever want to see her that close to an ax-wielding stranger again, even if said stranger is an innocent trail worker. The sight is just too damn unnerving.

A few more huffs and puffs, and we're back on the summit of Mount Osceola. A breeze rises up and over the exposed ledges, sweeping itself through our hair and drying the sweat from our foreheads. Alex lifts her face upward and gratefully smiles into the cool and refreshing air. She looks beautiful, standing there like that, angel-blonde remnants of last year's bangs fluttering on her forehead. For a moment, I can see the woman she will become—I can see what she'll look like in ten or fifteen years. Of course, as her mother, I could justifiably be accused of bias, but I think she's going to be one gorgeous female.

We throw our packs against a large cement block, a remnant of an old dismantled fire tower. The trail mix comes out, and we share handfuls, munching up the M&M's and sucking the salt from the almonds.

"Hey, Alex," I begin through a mouthful of raisins.

"What?" she asks, spraying me with chewed-up peanuts.

"You know that guy back there?"

"What guy?"

"What guy?" I think to myself in amazement.

"Um, the guy with the huge ax who stood right next to you while I climbed over the chimney."

"Oh, him. He was nice." Her hand goes back into the bag of trail mix. "Yuck," she exclaims as her hand reemerges. "Mostly raisins."

As I pick out the raisins, I cautiously ask, "How do you know he was nice?"

"I just know," Alex answers.

I chew my trail mix and wonder how to go about this. I don't want to sully my daughter's basic trust in human nature; I want her to see the good in people and not automatically suspect the bad. I also want her to learn to trust her instincts. If she feels strange about speaking to someone, then she shouldn't. If she feels comfortable with the person, then she should feel free to converse. As long as I'm right there beside her, of course.

The day is cloudy, but not overly so. Small wisps of gray float above the valley to our southeast. Alex gets up and walks over toward the edge of the summit's ledge; I instinctively rise and follow. The two of us stand, side by side, gazing out onto Waterville Valley. A large green hump is situated to our immediate northeast. It is East Osceola, the summit from whence we just came, looking like a giant green gumdrop thrown to Earth by some careless, sweet-toothed goddess. I stare at it and try to imagine the happy, half-naked ax-man blissfully roaming through its trees.

"Mama, it's like magic!" Alex joyfully exclaims,

and I return my attention to the valley. A wind has picked up, and several clumps of cloud are speedily moving in our direction, delicate poofs of vapor riding a current toward Osceola's ledge. They are level with our eyesight, and they rush toward us wildly. Alex and I goggle at them, enchanted. They're friendly gray ghosts coming to pay us a visit, zooming closer and closer until they reach the granite and whoosh up and over our heads. The last one doesn't whoosh like the others, but instead plows right into us, and we are momentarily immersed in a glorious fog. Then they are past, and the skies to the southeast are clear once again. Alex lets out a "whoo-hoo!" and I laugh with delight. Not wanting to interrupt this moment, I decide to shelve the ax-man discussion until later. We can talk about it during our descent.

The couple who passed us returns from their jaunt to East Osceola just as a group of five arrives from the parking area. Everyone sprawls out and snacks on their various goodies, enjoying the day and the plentiful views. Alex plays summit hostess, approaching everyone and initiating conversation. There are smiles all around as she cheerfully chatters away. I watch and admire my daughter's affability. How can I strike the correct balance when I speak to her? I don't want her to be afraid to do this, to walk around, greeting people happily and lovingly. This is part of the fun: sharing this wonderful experience with others is something she enjoys, and I don't want to take that away from her. So how do I tell her to be wary of people without stifling her natural positive attitude?

There's a golden Labrador up here; it offers a paw to Alex, who kneels and takes it immediately. For the next few minutes, the two immerse themselves in gestures of affection. Alex pets the dog, the dog licks Alex's face, the dog rolls on its back, Alex scratches its tummy. The owners smile and say a few soft words to Alex. She answers between fits of giggles. Eventually she returns to me, cheeks wet from the dog's kisses. One of the owners follows her and sits next to me, introducing himself as Jim.

"Your daughter tells me this isn't her first 4K," he begins in a pleasant tone.

"No, the Osceolas are numbers six and seven," I answer, my voice naturally full of maternal pride.

"That's amazing. She's quite the hiker."

"Yeah, she is," I agree.

Jim smiles and looks at Alex, who is busy digging a sandwich out from her pack. He is silent for a few moments, but the expression on his face indicates there's a question or comment imminent. Finally, he takes a breath and asks, "Your husband doesn't mind? You taking her up here alone, I mean?"

Fortunately, I bite my tongue and swallow my first response. This man is not trying to be offensive. I get the sense he is genuinely curious and truly does not realize how condescending that kind of a question really is.

I take a deep breath, then calmly reply, "Do you ask the same kind of question of fathers who hike with their sons?" My tone is not rude, for my intent is not to attack. If possible, I hope to open his mind a wee bit.

Jim looks startled, then turns red with embarrassment. "No, uh, good point," he sputters. He starts to rise, but I reach out my hand and touch his leg.

"Please stay. I didn't mean to make you feel awkward."

He pauses, then sits. As his face returns to a healthy shade of pink, he offers an apologetic explanation. "It's just that things can happen to a woman that don't usually happen to a man."

Alex is engrossed in her sandwich and, I hope, unaware of our conversation. I've enough to discuss with her on the way down; I don't want to have to add this layer of context.

Lowering my voice, I reply, "True. However, what are we supposed to do? Stay home? Only go when a man can come with us? That's an awfully limited way to live, and we're not all that fond of limits."

He smiles at me. It's an honest smile; there's nothing condescending in his expression. I smile back, then bid him adieu as he returns to his partner.

"What was that about?" Alex asks.

Rats. She was listening. Of course she was.

"That guy wondered why we didn't hike with Papa, or with another man. He thought it might be dangerous for us to hike by ourselves."

"Why?"

"In case a bad man saw us and wanted to hurt us."

"Can't a bad man hurt another man? Do bad men only hurt women?"

"Well, women are usually smaller than men, so we're picked on more often."

Alex looks me up and down, then states, "You're not smaller than a man."

She's right. I'm not exactly petite.

"Don't worry about it, Alex. All we need to do is be aware of who's around us. Also, we shouldn't tell anyone we're alone."

A wrinkle crosses my daughter's forehead. "People can *see* we're alone."

"Yes, but maybe they think we're with people who are just down the trail. We don't need to tell them there's no one behind us."

Time to begin the descent. Alex is ready; she's up and reaching for her backpack. I push myself to my feet.

"Just use your pepper spray if a bad guy comes along," Alex matter-of-factly instructs as she pulls her pack's straps over her shoulders. "I don't want to stay home. Just spray the guy in the face and we'll be fine." With that, she snaps her buckles and walks off.

That's my girl.

One mile later, I bring us back to our discussion about the ax-man. Feminist bravado aside, my daughter still needs to learn when to keep her distance from strangers.

I ask her again about the man with the ax, if she had any strange sense when she spoke with him, if she felt funny standing right next to him when she didn't know who he was. She insists he was a nice guy.

Though I'm a big believer in following your instincts, I explain that the few bad people in this world will sometimes pretend to be nice just to trick you into getting closer to them so that they can grab you.

Alex stops and looks up at me.

"That man was a bad person?"

"No," I quickly say. Then, "Well, maybe. I don't know."

Arg. I'm bungling this.

"Look," I begin, "we don't know that man. He was standing right next to you, and I didn't hear or see him coming. He had a large ax in his hand—it bothered me that he was standing so close to you without me there to protect you. He was probably a good guy—most people are—but the point is that we don't know him, so we can't be completely sure. So next time, if someone walks up to you and I'm not standing right there, and especially if I can't get to you right away, then take a few steps back."

Alex thinks on this for a while as we continue on

our way. I hope I haven't just made her paranoid of everyone she meets.

We hike the next mile or so with difficulty. Both of us are huffing and puffing; even usually peppy Alex seems to be wearing out. Though it felt like an easy climb on the way up, that side trip to East Osceola was probably more than we should have attempted. It felt much more difficult than our Eisenhower/Pierce trip. My feet begin to drag, and Alex asks for a water break. I happily sit and pull out my Nalgene bottles.

"Most people are good, right?" Alex asks after she drinks her fill.

"Yes, I believe so," I answer.

We rise, then fall into a long silence as we make our way down the boulder-strewn, slab-filled trail. It's not easy going; our legs ache, and the rocks are huge. There's nary a flat surface, and our feet continually bend and twist as we hike over the jagged stones.

"What about all those people at the top?" Alex eventually asks, butt-sliding down a particularly steep granite protuberance and landing lightly on the dirt below. "They were okay, right?"

"Yes," I respond, following Alex's lead and lowering myself until the seat of my pants touches rock. I don't slide as gracefully as my daughter, and my feet shakily hit the ground. I take a few hurried steps forward to keep my balance, then grab the trunk of a tree to bring myself to a halt.

"We were among many other people, and *you* approached each one of *them*. Also, I was close by and able to help if needed."

"What if one of them had grabbed me?"

"I would have jumped up, run over, and made that person let you go. Others would have helped too."

"What if that didn't work?"

"Then I would have sprayed the person in the face," I reply, smiling.

Alex snorts. "What if everyone had grabbed me, all at once?" she asks, her face lit up with silliness.

"Then I would have sprayed everyone in the face."

"Everyone?"

"Everyone. All at once."

Alex giggles.

We're very close to the car now, and I'm grateful to be near the end of our hike. I am exhausted and start to inwardly withdraw in an effort to conserve energy. Though my daughter must be at least equally tired, as she must take two or three steps to match every one of mine, she does not withdraw as I do. Instead, she sings, making up lyrics to spontaneous melodies. This is her way of reenergizing. I first noticed this delightful habit while descending Tecumseh, and I will continue to witness it throughout the remainder of our quest for the New Hampshire Forty-eight. Alex's method of pumping herself up is to talk, sing, hum, chant, or count out loud. During future hikes, I will often tell her to narrate an original story or sing on her own, anything to allow me to carefully measure my own energy expenditure while simultaneously allowing her the expression she so obviously needs.

For now, she is content to softly sing an original and spontaneous song. Her lyrics describe a frightened woman who tries to attack everyone she meets with pepper spray. My daughter happily bounces down the last few tenths of a mile, her chipper soprano ringing through the air.

Mistakes Can Have Serious Consequences

Hugh Tells a Cautionary Tale, August 2008

After only two months of weekend hiking, Alex and I have ascended nine peaks on the Four Thousand Footer list. We are checking off mountains much faster than I had originally anticipated. When I first envisioned the two of us tackling this quest, I figured it would take us at least four or five years to finish. If we keep to our current pace, however, we may reach our forty-eighth summit before Alex turns seven.

My daughter's consistent fortitude, determination, and enthusiasm lead me to believe that she will turn into quite the outdoorswoman. Her love for hiking is obvious. She describes her adventures to anyone who will listen, she molds mountains in her sandbox, she draws pictures of smiling stick figures standing on pointed summits.

Unfortunately, her gusto has become coupled with a dangerous sense of invincibility. During our last descent, Alex completely relaxed all her previous standards of caution. To my great concern, she continually skipped over rocks and jumped over slippery roots. She turned her head to talk to me while descending boulders. She twirled her hiking poles through the air with no concern as to who or what was behind her (I got whacked twice). Worst of all, she brushed aside my admonishments with the air of a doctor dismissing a hypochondriac's imagined symptoms.

I've never been one to hover over my children while they play. If they want to jump off rocks in the park, fine. If they want to climb trees and dangle from the branches, fine. If they want to run down a steep sidewalk, fine. I'm of the philosophy that kids need to define their own physical boundaries and develop their own gross motor skills. While at a playground, I allow them to do whatever they want, as long as they're mindful of the children around them.

In the Whites, however, things are very different. Little skips and jumps that are perfectly acceptable on a sidewalk are absolutely verboten on the trail. If Alex falls and injures herself, I will need to carry her for miles over extremely rough terrain. It will be, at best, a long, painful, and very unhappy experience.

Little kids don't usually have a sense of drastic consequences, especially when they're feeling strong and powerful. You can say, "Mind what you do or some awful thing might happen," but their brains won't really comprehend what you're telling them. It's finally beginning to dawn on young Alex that her abilities far surpass those of most others her age, and, unfortunately, she seems to think she must therefore be superhuman.

I'm happy she's proud of herself, but I want her to understand that she can break a leg just as easily as any other kid. She needs to speak with someone who has been in her position. Someone who was also a strong athlete at an incredibly young age. Someone who, in his youth, also thought he was indestructible—and ended up paying an enormous price for his overconfidence. She needs to see, with her own eyes, the potential consequences of split-second mistakes.

She needs to speak with her father. It's time for him to explain to his children exactly how he lost his legs.

I sit the girls down on the living room couch one evening and ask Hugh to tell them the story of his 1982 accident on Mount Washington. The same story he has told numerous times to journalists, nightly news reporters, and TV/film directors. The story that is well documented in Alison Osius's book, *Second Ascent*. He has told this story so many times and relived this tragedy for so many people . . . but tonight, the recounting will be unique. His audience won't be some stranger from NBC News, NPR, or ESPN. Instead, it will be his own beloved and adoring daughters.

The girls, being very young, have never inquired about the artificial limbs they sometimes help their father attach each morning. I suppose they've viewed his residual limbs as completely normal—some people have biological legs, and some don't. I'm not sure they've ever even realized that their father used to have human legs. They've just accepted what they've seen as the way things are and the way things always have been.

But now it's time. It will be upsetting, sure. But it's time. Alex needs to understand that she must take these mountains very, very seriously.

The girls sit on either side of Hugh and listen as he begins to talk in a quiet and gentle tone.

"When I was seventeen years old—" he begins.

"How old is that?" Alex interrupts.

"The girl across the street is seventeen," I say.

Alex thinks for a moment, apparently trying to visualize her father as young as our neighbor, then says, "Okay."

"When I was seventeen, a friend and I climbed Mount Washington in the wintertime."

"What month?" Alex asks.

"January," Hugh patiently answers. Neither of us discourages her interruptions, as we know she is only trying to create a more complete mental picture so that she might better understand.

"Why did you climb Mount Washington in January? Weren't you cold?" Alex asks.

"I did a lot of ice climbing back then. I started climbing ice when I was just a bit older than you are right now. I spent most of my childhood climbing mountains and ice."

Hugh is drastically understating his experience, but for the sake of our kids, it doesn't matter. They won't be able to comprehend the number of climbs and hikes he did before the age of seventeen. Hugh was considered a child prodigy in the rock and ice climbing community. He had his first set of crampons at age seven, and by age eight he had hiked 11,624-foot Mount Temple in the Canadian Rockies and attempted 14,411-foot Mount Rainier with his father and two older brothers. The weather on Mount Rainier forced them to turn back, but Hugh returned to the peak when he was eleven and reached the summit. During his childhood summer vacations to various mountain ranges, he pioneered climbs that precious few adults could handle. By the time he was sixteen, Hugh was the first to ascend some of the most difficult routes on the East Coast. The climbing community assumed he would go on to have a very famous and fruitful mountaineering career.

Then came the fateful trip up 6,288-foot Mount Washington. In January 1982, at the age of seventeen, Hugh and a friend, Jeff Batzer, decided to do an ice climb up O'Dell's Gully in Huntington Ravine. To minimize the risk of being struck by an avalanche, they dropped their packs at the base of the climb so they could ascend lightly and quickly. Their intent was to reach the top of the ice climb and then immediately descend.

"After my friend and I climbed the ice, we decided to walk a short distance toward the summit. It was windy and snowy, but we figured we'd just go a few hundred feet."

Hugh continues to speak in a measured voice, but I know this can't be easy for him. The decision to head toward Mount Washington's summit was a spontaneous one. Hugh is not and never has been a peakbagger. He's a climber. He likes to get to the top of a particular rock or ice climbing route, but he doesn't care all that much about touching the actual summit. It was such a casual decision on that cold and fateful day in 1982. So what if they didn't have all their gear? What could possibly happen? Why not walk for just a bit, even if the wind was starting to really blow?

Unfortunately, both boys failed to remember that they were not carrying compasses. Since their original plan was to ascend an ice gulley, they had left their compasses at home. After all, to turn back during a vertical climb, one simply goes down. Navigation isn't much of an issue. Once a person tops out from a climb and starts walking above tree line, however, the importance of a compass becomes paramount. The choices for movement now extend well beyond the simple up-down dichotomy. There are too many flat or moderately graded surfaces, and without clear visibility, it's easy to lose one's sense of direction. Up above the ice climb, in the region known as Mount Washington's Alpine Garden, they had only their eyesight to depend on. In the moment, this didn't seem like too much of a problem. They weren't trying to go all the way to the top, after all. Just a few minutes of hiking, maybe a few tenths of a mile at most. The risk appeared minimal.

"It was a cold and snowy day, and while we were walking, the wind became so strong that it almost knocked us over."

Sage and Alex's eyes grow wide.

"We decided to turn around—"

"Good thinking, Papa," Alex interrupts. She and Sage both look relieved. Odd, how the minds of children work. It's as though they expect him to tell us that all turned out well, that they came back down, went to a coffee shop, and drank some hot tea. Even as Hugh sits there with the bottom part of his sweatpants empty and dangling toward the floor.

"But we got into trouble," Hugh begins, and his voice becomes even more measured. "When we turned around, the wind was so bad that it blew snow all around us. We couldn't see where we were going. We almost couldn't see each other, even though we were walking side by side. We thought we went the right way, but we didn't. We ended up going down the wrong side of the mountain by accident."

Sage looks horrified. Tears well up in her eyes, and she asks in a very shaky voice, "Did you die, Papa?"

Hugh smiles reassuringly at her and answers, "No, honey."

Both girls relax a bit as they look their father over and verify that yes, he is right in front of them, and no, he did not die on that miserable winter day.

"How did you get back?" Alex asks.

"We didn't," Hugh says. "My friend and I were lost for three and a half days out in the cold woods. The temperatures were below zero—"

"Is that cold?" Alex asks.

"Yes, it's very cold. When it's that cold out, we don't let you play outside."

The girls look amazed. We almost never keep them indoors. On the contrary, they're usually the only kids in the neighborhood playing in the yard when the temperature dips below the freezing point.

"The snow went up to our waists and we didn't have any food or water with us."

"What about a tent?" Alex asks.

"No. We had left our backpacks at the bottom of the ice climb, since we thought we would come right back down. We didn't have anything with us."

"Were you scared?" Sage asks in a small voice.

"Yes," Hugh answers. "We were both terrified."

Hugh and Jeff had turned around within minutes of trying to walk toward the summit. However, in the very short amount of time it took for them to walk a couple of tenths of a mile, the wind speed had increased enough to create whiteout conditions. They could not see more than five feet in front of them, and they had to keep hold of each other so as not to become separated in the blinding, blowing snow. In Hugh's decade-plus of experience, he had never been on such a flat expanse while ascending a mountain. The whiteout conditions were impossible to navigate. Without the aid of a map or compass, the two boys did what most lost hikers tend to do: they turned their backs to the wind and began walking downward, toward where they thought they had ascended.

Their path of descent felt right at first, for the immediate gulley seemed similar in shape to the one they had climbed earlier. However, once below tree line, it was obvious they had gone the wrong way. Going back up was out of the question, however—they would most likely have ended up wandering about blindly in the whiteout with no idea of which direction to go, and the windchill would have quickly brought on frostbite and hypothermia. No, they had to keep descending through the trees. It was much safer this way, as the trees blocked most of the wind and therefore at least enabled the boys to see where they were headed. They were just going to have to try to walk out from where they were—which was, unfortunately, Mount Washington's extremely remote Great Gulf region.

"There was so much snow on the ground that we couldn't tell whether we were walking over a river or over land. Twice, I walked over a river by accident and my legs broke through the snow and sank into the water. My legs and feet got wet, and I didn't have any dry clothing to change into. Jeff helped me out of the river, and then we both tried to keep moving on."

Hugh is sugarcoating this a bit for the girls, and I don't blame him. Sage already looks aghast, and Alex's eyes are very wide indeed. The truth is, when Hugh punched through the river, he sank into fast-flowing, ice-cold water and barely avoided being swept under the ice by the river's current. Jeff extended his ice ax and saved Hugh, gradually pulling him out and away from the water.

"Where did you sleep?" Alex asks.

"We dug into the snow and made caves. We gathered fallen branches and lay down on top of them, to keep our bodies off the snow. Then we slept cuddled together, to try to keep each other warm."

The boys spent three nights in subzero temperatures and suffered through a blizzard. Their boots and socks became frozen clumps of ice, and pulling them on in the mornings became a severe challenge. Trying to fit rock-hard, frozen boots onto swollen, frostbitten feet was a torturous enterprise, and Hugh eventually gave up. Instead of boots, he wore his waterproof mittens over his toes. Though both boys did their best to keep moving, Hugh could take only one or two steps before falling over. The bones in his feet had frozen.

"How did you get home?" Sage asks, her knees drawn up underneath her chin, her arms around her ankles.

"We were lost for almost four days. On the last day, a lady was out snowshoeing and saw some tracks we had made in the snow. She followed them and found us. She went to get help, and we were taken to the hospital. My legs were so frozen that the doctors had to cut them off."

Sage, who has seen her father put on his artificial legs a countless number of times, gasps. Alex's eyes are full of tears, and she asks, "Did it hurt?"

"Yes," Hugh answers. "It didn't hurt during the operation, because I was asleep. But it hurt very badly for weeks and months afterward. Sometimes it still hurts, even now. Sometimes I feel like a part of my leg is still there, and it's painful."

It's a miracle both boys survived their ordeal. Hypothermia had set in, but never enough to make them forget the survival techniques they had learned as young children. They kept their mental faculties together enough to build snow caves, huddle together, and lie on branches instead of the snow. They did not let each other sleep because they were afraid they wouldn't wake up again. Many victims of hypothermia feel a warming sensation as they become closer and closer to death. These people often take off and discard their clothing, under the illusion that their bodies are hot when, in actuality, they are literally freezing to death. Though Hugh and Jeff were in the severe stages of hypothermia when they were rescued and brought into the hospital, neither one of them ever lost their sense of sanity while they were out there in the woods. Though Hugh remembers feeling warm at times, he always knew better than to take off any article of clothing. He was always well aware of the situation he was in.

"You're okay now, though, right? Most of the time?" Alex asks.

"Yes, most of the time I'm fine. However," Hugh pauses and looks from one daughter to the other, very seriously. I cannot imagine how it must feel for him to have to describe the rest of the story. For there's more, and what's coming next is far more horrific than anything he's already divulged.

"There was a group of rescue workers trying to find us while we were lost," Hugh begins. "Two of them were hit by an avalanche."

Alex raises her eyebrows, and Hugh realizes that the girls don't understand what that word means: *avalanche*. He gives them an explanation, and then continues. "One of the men was okay, but one of them wasn't. One of them was buried by the avalanche and pushed very quickly into a tree. His name was Albert Dow. Albert Dow was killed by that avalanche. Albert Dow died while he was trying to find and rescue me."

Hugh is remarkably calm as he states this. However, his tone is not casual, not in the least. He speaks in a low but firm voice and looks from one daughter to the other, making extended eye contact with each. I've no doubt Alex and Sage will remember these minutes for the rest of their lives.

Both girls are initially silent, and Hugh watches them patiently. Sage is the first to speak.

"Did the doctors fix him?"

"No," Hugh says firmly. "They couldn't fix him. He died. He can never come back."

I'm not sure Sage understands, as she's three and perhaps doesn't really have a full grasp of the concept of death. That's okay. Alex is the one I want this message to reach. She's the one going with me out there; she's the one who needs to comprehend. And she does. Her face is pale, and she's looking at her father with an expression of deep sadness. I wish I could get inside her brain and discover what she's thinking. Has her opinion of her beloved father changed? Does she have more respect for him now, or less? She'll never see him exactly the same way again. Every time he puts on or takes off his legs, she'll think of her father as a teenage boy, lost and near death, and of a young man she's never met, a brave fellow who died in an onslaught of rushing snow.

Hugh and Alex's eyes lock for a minute, and then Alex leans over and wraps her arms around her father. Sage, following her sister's cue, does the same. The three of them stay like that for a while, one warm mass of family huddled together on the couch. I remain still in my chair, not wanting to interrupt. Eventually, Alex releases her hold, rises, and silently leaves the room.

After his accident, Hugh created his own artificial legs, specially built for climbing, and went right back into the sport. Within a year, he was climbing ice and rock better than he ever had with biological legs. On his self-fashioned limbs, he pioneered extremely advanced routes, and he regained his previous status as one of the nation's best climbers. Eventually, he went to college and graduate school, getting his master's degree at the Massachusetts Institute of Technology (MIT) and his PhD at Harvard. He is now a tenured professor at MIT, where he invents and builds advanced robotic prostheses.

Alex's careless jumps and skips cease immediately. Her father has gotten through to her. Good. One split-second decision, made on a whim, one that seems completely innocent and of minimal risk at the time, can have life-changing—or life-ending—results.

Divide and Conquer

Peaks #10 and #11: Mount Monroe and Mount Washington,
August 28–29, 2008

Thankfully, Alex's ascent of Mount Washington is nothing like her father's. There are no accidents; we don't lose our way; and instead of traveling light, I carry a pack that weighs approximately the same poundage as an obese elephant.

Conquering 6,288-foot Mount Washington means breaking the hike into two Alex-friendly days. Ascending and descending within the same twenty-four hours might be more than my daughter can handle, as the elevation gain and mileage are greater than anything she has yet accomplished. We therefore decide to take advantage of the Appalachian Mountain Club's Lakes of the Clouds hut, one of the highest and most popular of the AMC's backcountry overnight facilities.

Lakes of the Clouds rests a moderate 1.5 miles southwest of Mount Washington's summit. Mount Monroe's craggy peak rises just a half mile from the hut's front door. Alex and I will be able to bag two of New Hampshire's highest mountains with relative ease, thanks to the conveniently located accommodations.

While planning our trip, Alex tells me that spending the night above tree line on the shoulder of the Northeast's tallest mountain is an experience our entire family should share. I agree, and the two of us ask Hugh and Sage if they'd like to join us. Normally, they wouldn't be able to, since Sage isn't yet capable of hiking that great a distance, and her weight is too much for Hugh to comfortably handle for more than nine miles of rocky terrain. However, for this particular peak, the trip will be a piece of cake.

Mount Washington, being the prominent mountain that it is, attracts tourists like sugar attracts ants. Its popularity therefore offers a New Hampshire peak experience unlike any other. Instead of hiking, one can drive to the summit, or take a special train called the Cog Railway. Once at the top, one can visit two museums, a weather observatory, a restaurant, and a gift shop.

While all this man-made clutter appears strange in the midst of an otherwise barren and rocky landscape, it does present nice possibilities for those who are less inclined or able to ascend on their own two feet. For our family, the existence of the Mount Washington Auto Road is extremely convenient. It will enable the four of us to turn this peakbagging adventure into a family outing. Alex and I will hike up the west side of the mountain using the incredibly steep Ammonoosuc Ravine Trail while Hugh and Sage drive up the northeast side of the mountain on the Auto Road. The Ammonoosuc Ravine Trail ends a few dozen feet from Lakes of the Clouds' front door; Alex and I will claim our family's bunks while Hugh and Sage descend the moderate mile and a half down Mount Washington's summit cone. At some point Alex and I will ascend Mount Monroe; then all four of us will spend the night at the hut before hiking up Mount Washington's peak the next morning. Hugh and Sage will then return to the valley by car, while Alex and I descend the mountain on foot.

The big day arrives. The kids greet the morning with excited cheers, but Hugh and I are subdued. What if Mount Washington's notoriously unpredictable weather takes a nasty turn? The forecast looks favorable, but it looked favorable the morning we first attempted Mount Tom, and I remember how that turned out.

Hugh and I come to a last-minute understanding before leaving the house: if, after arriving at the summit, the winds are too high, the temperatures are too low, and/or the clouds look too ominous, then he and Sage will not descend to Lakes of the Clouds but will instead head right back down the mountain in the safety of the car. Alex and I will either turn around at the first sign of atmospheric trouble, or we'll quicken our pace toward the hut, depending on where we happen to be at the time. Hugh and I will use our communication radios to give each other status reports throughout the day.

Hugh and Sage drop off Alex and me at the Ammonoosuc Ravine Trail around 8:00 in the morning, which, in my personal opinion, is the perfect time to begin. We have all day to hike the three miles to the hut, so there is no rush and no pressure on either me or my daughter. We can take as many breaks as Alex needs.

The first mile is flat and pleasant; the narrow path winds through a dense forest, leading to a picture-perfect brook. Turning right, we easily walk the second mile, which is also flat, never leaving the sight and sound of the noisy water. At one point we notice a little dam of tumbled, gnawed-up logs; Alex guesses that this is the work of beavers. We linger for a while, hoping to catch sight of a little big-toothed architect, but no such critter emerges. We eventually continue onward, enjoying the peaceful morning and easy stroll.

Before we know it, we're at Gem Pool: a lovely, liquid oasis that marks the end of our level walking. A small waterfall cascades down the rocky mountainside and crashes into the little round body of water. Every few seconds, an errant drop falls outside the pool and splats onto a bordering rock. It's a pleasant place, perfect for our first rest break and a little snack.

As Alex sits and eats, I verbally prep the two of us for the climb ahead. According to the guidebooks, the final mile of this trail, from the point where we currently sit all the way up to the hut, is extremely steep. There will be many boulders to scramble and many rock steps to climb. Alex listens intently but does not appear daunted. She tells me she's up to it. After all, it's just a mile.

The guidebooks are accurate; it is a steep and unrelenting ascent! Nevertheless, our spirits are high as our hands repeatedly slap rock and our feet struggle to find purchase on bare and near-vertical surfaces.

As we gain altitude, the trees shorten and thin until we are treated to a clear view down into the valley. The sight is breathtaking. We can see for miles, and there's barely a cloud in the sky. A light breeze dries the sweat from our faces, and we smile deliriously at each other, the impact of Mother Earth's beauty hitting us just as hard as it did when we first stepped above tree line on Mount Eisenhower.

The trail is now more rock climb than hiking path, so we take our time and stop for breaks frequently. I welcome the breathers whenever Alex requests them, which is not as often as I'd like. My daughter possesses an overflowing well of energy, and I envy it. She does need rest breaks, of course, but when she rises afterward, she usually acts as though her batteries have been fully recharged. The same force that prevents her from sitting still during our schoolwork time works well to her advantage out here.

There are a final few slabs of rock to conquer, and then we see Lakes of the Clouds just above us. Alex lets out a victory "yay!" and grins from ear to ear. The view toward the hut is simply magnificent. To our immediate right 5,372-foot Mount Monroe rises in a tall, pointy bump, and the tip of Mount Washington stands majestically a mile and a half to our left. Our vigor renewed by the prospect of hot chocolate and a comfortable bench, we jog up the trail and skip around the hut until we stand in front of its entrance. I snap a triumphant picture of Alex and feel my shoulders relax. The most difficult part of our day is over.

Myriad backpacks litter the flat ground in front of the hut's front door. Hiking poles rest in angles, propped up against various rocks and boulders. There's

a short stone wall along the front of the building; a half dozen pairs of smelly socks adorn its surface. Alex and I untangle ourselves from our pack straps and are just about to leave our belongings next to a particularly smooth boulder when I hear the crackling of static at my hip. "Trish . . . ?" It's Hugh contacting me by radio. He and Sage have reached the summit and are now making their way down the 1.5 miles to the hut. The day is windless and clear; they have absolutely beautiful weather in which to make their journey. A day like this on Mount Washington is reportedly rare, and I give silent thanks to Mother Earth for keeping herself calm while my husband and three-year-old daughter make their way down the giant exposed summit.

Since there's at least an hour to kill before Hugh and Sage arrive, Alex and I enter the hut and register our family for the evening.

Built out of wood and run on solar and wind power, Lakes of the Clouds offers an illusion of roughing it at high elevation. The overnight guest is served a three-course homemade dinner before retiring for the evening to a bunk draped with three warm woolen blankets (there are six to fifteen bunks per room, stacked three and four beds high). A hearty breakfast is served the next morning at 7:00 a.m., and then guests are expected to fold their bunk's blankets before leaving for their next destination. To a seasoned hiker, spending the night at Lakes of the Clouds is a luxury; for those hundreds of tourists looking for a unique alpine experience, Lakes is looked upon as a backcountry novelty. For us, it will be both. A luxury, because we'll get to eat and sleep very well while bagging a couple of peaks. A backcountry novelty, because, well, we've never done this before.

After our gear is stowed by our bunks, Alex and I exit the hut to lie about and soak in some sunshine. We sprawl for a while and stare at the blue sky, stretching our legs and relishing the feel of warm stone on our backs. Eventually, Alex tires of being still, so I give her my camera and allow her to go at it. She snaps pictures of the little windmill on top of the roof, my hiking poles, her feet (which have been temporarily freed from the bondage of her boots), and the door that leads to the "Dungeon," a small room separate from the rest of the hut. Lakes of the Clouds is closed, boarded, and vacant from October through May; I've read that the Dungeon is kept unlocked for winter hikers who find themselves caught in foul weather and unable to descend to the valley below. It's not an advertised space, and it's not meant to be used except in times of emergency. Alex asks if we can take a look inside, but the door is closed, and I have the feeling we should leave it be.

Alex finishes snapping her photos, and we continue to rest happily. We watch the clouds float over our heads, we look down and out at the trees far below, we look at our map and try to name all the mountains we can see. It's a perfect piece of time. I'm glad we have this opportunity to just sit and not have to worry about getting back down to the car. The hut is a nice option. Breaking up this hike was the right thing to do. Even if Alex was capable of doing the entire thing in one day, it would be a shame to have to head back down to the valley after having just ascended on such a beautiful morning. It's simply too lovely out here to have to return to a place of low elevation.

An hour passes and we turn our heads toward Mount Washington, searching for two familiar silhouettes. Finally we see two figures coming toward us, one tall, one very short, both dressed in black. The tall person ambles with a seemingly casual gait, the result of walking on artificial legs and feet. The shorter figure hops and bops, exuding an energy only youth can generate. They draw nearer, and Alex shouts, "Papa! Sage!"

Sage raises her head and runs toward us, sailing over several jagged rocks with each hurried stride. Alex runs toward Sage, feet pounding in quick succession. They collide about thirty feet from the hut and knock each other over; then they roll in the dirt and giggle madly while Hugh smiles and tells me that Sage walked the entire way down on her own two feet.

After leaving Hugh's pack inside with the rest of our gear, the four of us take advantage of the rare and peaceful weather by staying outside as long as we can. I procure a few children's books from the hut's tiny "library" (a few shelves near the main eating area), and the four of us sit in the sun, beautiful scenery at our feet, together as a family. It's wonderful—for about sixty seconds. I am halfway through the second page of Dr. Seuss's *The Lorax* when the bickering begins.

Have you ever noticed how differently your children behave when they're not around each other? Don't get me wrong—I'm a huge proponent of family time and of nurturing sisterly/brotherly bonds. We are home-schoolers, after all, so my girls spend most of their waking hours together, or at least within proximity of each other. Though they usually get along very well and consider themselves best friends, squabbles are a normal and common part of our existence. Glorious phrases such as "Stop it" and "Don't look at me!" can be found floating through the air of our home at least three or four times a day.

Get each of them alone, however, spend a large chunk of time with just one, without the other, and you see an entirely different side of your child. Alex, for example, is a mature, happy, focused, and incredibly wise human being. That's easily apparent just by talking with her—when she's without her little sister. Sage is a sweet, intuitive, deep, and loving soul who wants nothing more than to talk with you for hours—when she's without Alex. Put the two of them together, and you get two kids who routinely act up and vie for their parents' attention. They love each other, no doubt, yet they engage in sibling rivalry nonetheless. Therefore, the quality of individual parent-child interaction is usually higher when Hugh and I take turns being with each daughter alone.

I'm up to where the first Thneed has been produced when Alex and Sage start accusing each other of breathing too hard. By the time the last Truffula tree has been chopped down, each daughter is glaring, and both are making rude faces at each other. I decide that now's a good time for Alex and me to bag Mount Monroe. I ask Sage if I can read the rest of the story to her when we return. She agrees, and Alex and I take off while Hugh starts a different book with Sage.

The summit's only five-tenths of a mile away; we reach it quickly and easily. Alex climbs onto the highest rock and sits. The mountain breeze gently lifts her hair from her forehead, and the sun's light intensifies the sky-blue color of her eyes; she sits with her knees drawn up to her chest, looking calm, looking peaceful. The two of us spend a few minutes taking in the stunning 360-degree views.

Alex asks to use my camera, and I hand it over. She takes myriad photographs, capturing the shapes and outlines of Mount Franklin, rising close to our southwest, and of Mount Washington, huge and domineering to our northeast. She clicks away at the glistening surface of the two small bodies of water lying near the hut (the "lakes of the clouds" after which the hut is named). A half mile immediately downward and to our east, we see the broad outline of the Gulfside Trail guiding a handful of hikers northward. As Alex points the camera toward the travelers, a few words of their conversation float up to our ears. I recognize the words *great, hut,* and *Washington.* The rest is a jumble of jovial noise.

Alex hands the camera back to me with a smile, her spat with Sage completely forgotten. She is her usual congenial self when we return to the hut.

Now it's time to snuggle with my youngest. I take Sage outside for the rest of *The Lorax* while Alex plays cards with Hugh. I treasure this time with my littlest daughter; her warm, compact little body rests against my side as I hold the book in front of us. After I read the final page, she climbs onto my lap, and we share a happy silence as the sun slowly sinks toward the horizon.

The evening meal is served by five college-age men and women who are loud, purposely comical, and friendly. The ninety guests of the hut sit family-style on benches around ten large wooden tables. The "croo," as the hut workers are called, dish out a hearty and homemade meal, starting with vegetable soup. Next comes a colorful salad, followed by a hot turkey dinner complete with mashed potatoes and green beans. This is hiker food; this is the stuff that nourishes those who walk up mountains. Full as I am after the main course, I make room for the chocolate-chip confection that is dessert. Yum.

The girls have eaten their fill, and both look as though they are going to pass out on their crumb-filled plates. I bundle them off to their bunks and tuck them in; Alex is asleep in four seconds, Sage in five. I crawl into a bunk across from them and immediately follow suit.

Alex and Sage are extremely happy the next morning, their mood bright after their enjoyable hut experience. They talk of the short, silly sketch the croo performed after breakfast: a strange, costumed fairy tale that served as a tutorial on the proper way to fold the hut's blankets. My two daughters laugh with each other as we pass between the two lakes . . . but soon Sage's pace diminishes to a speed too slow for Alex's liking. Hugh and I agree to separate and meet at the top. Alex and I skip ahead while Sage takes her time walking up the summit cone, patient Hugh by her side.

The Crawford Path between Lakes of the Clouds and Mount Washington's summit is well constructed and easy to follow. Large and carefully built stone cairns adorn the sides of the trail every few dozen feet, improving the path's visibility during fog or blowing snow. The grade feels moderate most of the way, and the two of us make quick progress, slowing only when we come to the trail's last, steep section. We huff and puff our way to the plateau that marks the summit area, and . . . oh my goodness.

It's 10:15 on a Sunday morning atop New Hampshire's highest mountain, but it looks like a Saturday afternoon in Boston. There are structures all over the place! We walk into the largest one, the Sherman

Adams Summit Building, which houses a cafeteria, a weather observatory, a museum, a post office, public restrooms, a gift shop, and an information desk staffed by a park ranger. There's a small crowd in here, mostly people sporting shorts and T-shirts and exhibiting a profound lack of sweat. Alex and I, both dressed in our base layers and carrying backpacks and hiking poles, are the recipients of many a stare as we amble about. I hear more than one person gasp, "Did that kid hike up?" I'm a bit put off by the degree of their amazement. Alex and I are now used to people looking surprised when they see us coming on the trail. These tourists who ascended using the Auto Road or the Cog Railway, however, are outright flabbergasted. Perhaps it's because they themselves don't hike, so they think such an activity is outright impossible for a small child? Alex and I do not stay inside for long, for we both feel odd under the gaze of so many eyes.

The next building we explore is the restored Tip Top House, a hotel that sheltered overnight guests in the mid-1800s. Now a museum (separate from the one in the Summit Building), it displays the kind of accommodations summit visitors experienced one and a half centuries ago.

The Tip Top House is close to the actual high point of Mount Washington, so the obligatory summit shot on top of "the rock pile" is next on our agenda. It's more than a bit odd, having our picture taken on this summit. We stand not only in the midst of buildings that don't seem as though they should be here, but also tourists who, in Alex's words, cheated. These people drove cars; they rode the Cog Railroad—in short, they didn't put forth any effort. Yet they want their picture taken on the high point all the same. Alex and I stand in line, balancing ourselves on the rocks, full of righteous indignation and feelings of superiority. A small part of my brain recognizes that we're being snobs, but the rest of me doesn't care. We should be allowed to cut in front of all those who rode up here. We hiked the entire distance, so why do we have to wait behind the drivers? Finally, it is our turn, and the picture is taken. Excellent. Now all we have to do is wait for Hugh and Sage so we can say our good-byes before hiking down into the valley.

We wander around the Auto Road's Stage Office, the upper terminus of the Cog Railway, and the FM radio transmitters, then head back to the Crawford Path to sit and wait. Just a minute or so later, Sage's head pops up over the immediate curve of the mountain, and Alex lets out an excited shriek. Sage sees Alex and grins widely. The two run toward each other and, just as they did outside Lakes of the Clouds, collide and knock each other over. They giggle madly and hug each other as they lie on the ground, acting as though they haven't seen each other in months. Those two—they're either in each other's arms or on each other's nerves. Normal sibling behavior, I guess.

Hugs and kisses are exchanged all around; then

Alex and I begin our long descent via the Gulfside and Jewell Trails. It's an onerous and, quite frankly, pain-in-the-butt hike. The Gulfside Trail is a literal jumble of giant rocks that we must step on and over very, very carefully. Some of these miniature boulders are loose and wobble beneath our feet. Others are solid, but piled at strange angles. The occasional cairn is all that marks the way; there is no obvious path to follow. We are forced to walk with our heads down, constantly watching our every step.

The rocks stretch out for miles, running the distance between Mount Washington and its four immediate neighboring peaks to the north: Mount Clay, Mount Jefferson, Mount Adams, and Mount Madison. We are small and insignificant in this barren landscape, and once again I thank Mother Earth for keeping the weather in check. I would not want to be out here during a thunderstorm.

The beginning of the Jewell Trail is more jumbled rock, and I start to grumble. When will we see a packed-dirt path? We stop for a while and rest. The day is clear and the scenery is beautiful, but I'm really tired and would like to be back at the car. Alex is doing well and isn't complaining, but I know she must be tired too. We've three miles to go, and again I reflect on the convenience of Lakes of the Clouds. Alex and I aren't yet ready to do this kind of hike all in one day.

A million years and many weary bones later, we reach the valley and climb into our car, dirty, smelly, and proud of ourselves. Upon returning home, I imme-diately investigate how many other long-distance hikes we can break into two or more pieces by using the hut system. Luckily, quite a few. During the months that follow, Alex and I stay at several other huts in order to tackle some of the more difficult mountains. We also make use of backcountry shelters and campsites. Alex and I enjoy our overnight adventures, and Alex learns that any distance is attainable if you break the journey into bite-size pieces.

"Happiness Is Only Real When Shared"
—*Christopher McCandless*

Autumn 2008

Alex and I are a mother-daughter team. Our first sixteen peaks were hiked without company, save for the ascent up Washington's summit cone with Sage and Hugh. We've been on our own for three reasons: (1) we haven't yet socialized with other hikers; (2) for safety purposes, I don't request trail companionship on the hiking forums, since telling hundreds of complete strangers our future whereabouts infringes upon my sense of safety; and (3) Alex's pace is too slow for the vast majority of 4K—that is, adult—hikers. I don't mind this relative isolation, since time spent alone with my daughter strengthens the bond between us. However, I do notice that every time someone passes us on the trail, Alex perks up and quickens her pace. I can see that she might enjoy this experience even more if she were in the company of other people.

For Alex's benefit, I begin looking for opportunities

to meet other outdoor enthusiasts. Fall arrives, and a "family hiking" trip up Mount Cardigan is announced on one of the Internet hiking forums. Excellent. Mount Cardigan is not a Four Thousand Footer, but it's a good-size peak and one that I think Sage might be able to handle. We mark the date on our calendar and let the organizer know that the three of us will be coming. Hugh will unfortunately be away that weekend, but I don't mind taking the girls by myself.

The day arrives, and we show up at the appointed campground with full backpacks and high spirits. Alex cheerfully introduces herself to those already gathered, then sits on a log to wait for those who have not yet turned up. I smile at everyone and give them my name, then try to pry Sage off my legs. She's shy around strangers and spends the next ten minutes glued to my side as the group waits for last-minute stragglers. Eventually the man who organized this get-together—a tall, affable fellow who goes by the name of "McRat"—declares it time to get moving. We're to take the Holt Trail, then the Clark Trail; it will be a mellow 2.5-mile ascent for Alex, but a challenging climb for Sage. I reassure my youngest that I will carry her when needed, but the presence of the other hikers seems to infuse Sage with extra chutzpah, and she insists that she will make it up there on her own two feet. Admiring her determination, I tell her that I know she's strong enough to accomplish such a goal, but my arms will be ready for her if she changes her mind.

We start our ascent in the company of four other adults and two older girls, ages eleven and twelve. Alex is thrilled; she is completely ecstatic. She keeps pace with the tweens and happily converses with them, apparently unaware that she's six and seven years younger than the taller kids who walk beside her. The older girls are kind to Alex and listen to her constant chatter as she bounces along. I walk behind the group with Sage, who holds my hand and steps slowly but steadily. The group hikes ahead, then sits and waits for Sage and me to catch up, then goes ahead again, then sits and waits. It's a pleasant, relaxed ascent. Everyone seems content to take it slowly and enjoy one another's company. Alex has a grand time, sometimes hiking with Sage and me, but mostly hiking in the midst of her new friends, each of whom treats her as a peer in spite of her young age. It is an enriching experience, one that demonstrates how much more can be added to a hike when in the presence of fine company.

We break out of the woods and encounter a handful of bare, sloping ledges. These are the final obstacles to overcome before reaching the actual summit. Sage is exhausted but proud of herself. Alex hops and bops as if she had just walked a few blocks instead of a couple of miles. We all climb the ledges together, as a group, and reach the top without incident.

Having a summit to oneself is a beautiful thing. One can sit and listen to the silence, feel the wind, and connect with one's Higher Power. It's a priceless sensation, and some people refuse to hike with others because they feel they must have that experience during each and every hike.

Sharing a summit, however, is also a beautiful thing. I sit, look around me, and smile at what I see. An adult from our group has whipped out a blue and yellow kite from her backpack and is flying it over the valley below. Alex and Sage are giving some of their Goldfish crackers to the tweens, who in turn share some of their sandwiches. McRat is immersed in cheerful conversation with someone he met two seconds ago. Everyone is joyful, everyone is pleased, everyone is sharing their positive energy with everyone else. The best parts of human nature are on display up here.

The girls come over and ask for the trail mix. We sit together for a while, the girls picking out bits of food they don't like and placing the morsels on my outstretched leg. My knee is soon covered in raisins from Alex, my shin in peanuts from Sage. Once the girls have sufficiently weeded their snack, they leave me and return to the tweens. I pick their rejected items from the fabric of my pants and pop them into my mouth, too engrossed in my noshing to notice the arrival of another member of our party. Only after I hear an unfamiliar voice comment on the day's clear sky do I look up and see a tall, fifty-something-year-old man with salt-and-pepper hair, standing a few feet away from me and talking with McRat. He is wearing a kilt.

My eyes are immediately drawn to this odd bit of clothing (how could they not be?). The dark green material flutters lightly in the breeze, sometimes whooshing up to reveal the black hiking shorts he sports underneath. The newcomer sees me looking, smiles, and introduces himself as MadRiver. My cheeks turn red, and I feel as though I've been caught looking up someone's skirt. Oh, wait a minute—I have. I mumble my own introduction and point out my daughters. He nods when I finish, then turns and continues his conversation with McRat. He disappears after a few minutes, and I don't see him again until we return to the campground.

Our descent is a slow one because of Sage's fatigue. She refuses to let me carry her, so we take tiny, slow steps and soon fall behind the rest of the group. Eventually, I tell everyone to go ahead and hike all the way down, that the girls and I will meet them at the campground later. Alex asks if she can go ahead with everyone else. McRat insists that Alex's company would be their pleasure, so I give my permission. The group disappears down the trail, Alex happily skipping alongside the adults.

By the time Sage and I make it down, there's a fire going, and Alex is consuming marshmallows by the handful. I congratulate Sage on her accomplishment, then sit her next to Alex and place half a Hershey's bar on her lap. Sage is completely worn out, but very proud of herself, as she should be; five miles up and down Mount Cardigan is a lot for a three-year-old to handle. I leave the kids to their candy and join the adults, who are engaged in animated conversation about various New Hampshire mountains and trails. One person keeps to himself, however. MadRiver sits on a folding chair and sips from his water bottle, gazing into the fire. I make my way over to him and say hello.

There's a second or two of silence; then he says, still staring into the fire, "Your kids are interesting. I've read the trip reports you post on the Internet. Alex is . . . different."

"Yes, she is," I respond. He's referring to the blog I created a few months ago. When it became apparent that Alex was probably going to hike 4Ks on a consistent basis, I created a blog that featured online pictorial essays of our adventures. *Trish and Alex Hike the 4000 Foot Whites* (www.trishandalex.blogspot.com) was my way of sharing our travels with my extended family and the online hiking community. I'd often include links to our posts within certain hiking forums; these always received favorable responses and plenty of supportive comments. Every once in a while, I'd get an irate private message telling me that the 4K peaks were no place for small children. These diatribes were infrequent, rarely written in a coherent manner, and easy to dismiss.

Later, after eating our fill of toasted marshmallows under a brilliant, star-filled sky, the girls and I are zipping up our coats and stepping away from the campfire when one of the other adults, an especially outgoing and friendly woman, asks if I can step aside with her for a moment. The girls sit on a boulder while she and I take a few steps into the woods.

"There's something you should know about that one," the woman says, her voice low and secretive, as she gestures toward MadRiver. The kilted man still sits by the fire, a hundred feet away. "He doesn't like children."

Um, okay. What does that mean? What am I supposed to do with this information? "Are my kids safe around him?" I ask, not knowing what else to say.

"Oh—oh yes, nothing like that," she looks down at her feet, flustered. "It's just that, well, he can be kind of gruff with them."

"Doesn't he have kids? Today's hike was supposed to be for people with kids, right?"

She raises her eyes to meet mine, an intense and earnest expression on her face. "No, he doesn't have kids. He came because he's a friend of McRat's. He met us at the top so he wouldn't have to hike up with a bunch of children. Some of us refer to him as 'the child hater.'"

I stand there, not knowing how to respond. The child hater? Really? Am I supposed to keep my kids away from this guy? What would happen if Alex accidentally bumped into him? Would he yell at her?

Smack her upside the head? And why is she telling me this now, right before we leave? Wouldn't this information have been useful much earlier in the day? Before I can ask any of these questions, the woman turns and quickly walks back to the fire. I take the girls and leave the campground in a state of utter befuddlement.

Deciding that it's safe to post our plans on the "members only" section of one Internet hiking forum, I let folks know of our upcoming ascent of 4,500-foot Mount Garfield. There are no responses to my announcement, so I assume it will just be the usual two of us tromping our way toward the summit.

The morning begins with a bit of a mystery. When we arrive at the trailhead, the parking lot is completely full. It's 7:00 a.m., the time Alex and I usually start, a time when most other hikers are just rolling out of their beds. We are used to arriving at a near-empty lot— why is there no place to park today? I leave my car off the road, across from the lot, and hope there's no ticket waiting on its windshield later this evening.

It's a scenic autumn morning. Alex and I crunch our way through the fallen leaves, admiring the reds, yellows, and browns. Gone is summer's greenery. Gone also are summer's little nuisances. There are no bugs, no sweaty armpits, no hot foreheads. We breathe the delightfully crisp autumn air and walk through the near-barren trees.

Our ramble is an easy one, in spite of the five-mile distance from car to summit, since the trail stays cooperatively moderate in grade. We are clipping along at a solid pace and are only a few tenths of a mile from the peak when the first jogger crosses our path.

There are more than a dozen in all, and they follow one another in rapid succession. Dressed in regular nylon shorts and tennis shoes, they are an odd addition to the typical mountain vista. We move out of their way in amused bewilderment, Alex's eyes opening wide. We haven't seen anyone run down a mountain trail before. I marvel at how gracefully they move. How do they run over these rocks without twisting their ankles?

Our confusion increases when we reach the top of Mount Garfield and see a giant penguin standing on the summit. Or rather, a man dressed as a penguin. He greets us by waving a large and fuzzy wing.

"What the . . . ?" Alex says, laughing. My thoughts exactly.

"We're part of an intercollegiate race," the penguin explains. "College kids are running up neighboring Mount Galehead, across the ridge, and then down Mount Garfield."

Though the wind is cold and blowing, we linger to watch the energetic, underdressed dynamos whiz by. Alex chats with the penguin, and he offers her some hot chocolate from a thermos sitting on a nearby boulder.

When it's time to descend, Alex is sky-high. "That was great!" she shouts as we make our way down the first rocky few tenths of a mile. Her euphoria increases more than I think possible when we suddenly hear a voice holler, "This must be Trish and Alex!"

An exuberantly jovial man and a more reserved, smiling woman stand a few dozen feet down the trail. They stride toward us with quick and confident gaits, and I take an instinctive (but unnecessary) step toward Alex. Within seconds, my hand is being grasped and powerfully shaken.

"Nice to meet you," the man booms. Then, to Alex, he says, "I've read all about your hikes. What a tough kid you are! We were hoping to meet you today!"

Alex's grin takes over her entire face.

The couple, avid White Mountain hikers, briefly depart to tag the summit, then quickly catch up to us during our descent. As we continue downward, the outgoing woman from Mount Cardigan, the one who warned me about MadRiver, comes up the trail, greets us, and declares that she too hopes to hike down with young Alex.

My daughter's self-esteem skyrockets, and she happily walks the rest of the way down the trail with her three new hiking buddies. It's obvious that Alex's joy is increased to the nth degree if she can share her appreciation of nature with other people.

From this point forward, I attempt to include others during our quest for the 4Ks. My efforts are rarely met with success, however, as Alex and I have our boots on the trail long before most get out of bed, and Alex's pace is far slower than that of the average adult hiker. Everyone we meet likes Alex and enjoys her company, but few choose to get up before dawn and hike at a speed that is too slow for their comfort. We do, however, manage to secure companionship for a good handful of future ascents. There is one person who becomes our most trusted hiking partner and a constant source of moral support: the kilt-wearing "child hater," MadRiver.

Though I am less of an extrovert than my daughter, I too take pleasure in hiking with others. The hiker whose company I most prefer, of course, is Alex. This realization hits home the first time I hike by myself.

Faced with the prospect of spending hours walking through cold drizzle, Alex decides to stay home one weekend with Hugh and Sage. When I ask if she minds if I go ahead and hike without her, she looks at me suspiciously for a few moments before granting her permission. She does, however, issue one caveat: I am not to hike anything "new," anything we haven't yet ascended. Respecting her wishes, I choose to tackle 5,716-foot Mount Jefferson, a mountain we've already crossed off our list.

Alex and I had taken the Caps Ridge Trail when

we climbed this peak, so, wishing for a bit of variety, I choose a different route for my solo adventure. I'll take Caps Ridge to the Link Trail, then take the Link to the Castle Trail, which will take me up Mount Jefferson's northwest face.

The beginning bit of Caps Ridge Trail is as I remember, with one startling exception. I don't have a small person commenting on the beauty of various natural details. I walk across some planks of wood, and no one tells me how interesting my footsteps sound. If there are flowers next to the path, I don't see them, because I'm not the one who notices such things when Alex and I hike. No one laughs when I walk into an early morning spiderweb that stretches across the trail. It is incredibly quiet. Too quiet. I miss my hiking partner.

My melancholy somewhat diminishes when I reach the Link Trail. This is something new, something I haven't seen before, something that might take my mind off of Alex's absence.

The *AMC White Mountain Guide* describes the Link Trail as heavily eroded, with difficult footing. As I slowly step my way along this mess of a path, I realize that the description is a huge understatement. Though the trail does not significantly ascend or descend, it is overgrown and completely falling apart. Countless times I put my hiking poles on what looks like solid ground, only to have that bit of trail crumble beneath my feet and slide down the mountain. Trees are overturned everywhere, and I have to climb over many root systems. I step on boulders, big ones with trail blazes on them, and they go toppling over and off the path. There are countless animal dens around and underneath the trail. The path itself is narrow, and tree branches grow over its middle. I give up avoiding sharp limbs and spiderwebs after the first half mile and re-sign myself to coming off the trail covered with dead insects and bloody scratches.

Though I am glad Alex doesn't have to deal with these nuisances, I can't help but wonder what she'd think of all this. Would she have as much trouble as I am having, hopping from solid piece of ground to rock, jumping off of boulders as they start to slide? The mother in me is relieved I don't have to worry about her safety out here. The adventurer in me recognizes that my daughter, a fellow adventurer, might find this trail exciting.

My ponderings are interrupted by a most unfor-tunate event. As I step over an impossibly large and gnarled root system, my camera slips out of my open front pocket, falls to the ground, slides down some loose dirt, and drops into a giant hole. Crap.

Off goes my pack and out comes my headlamp. My beam of light illuminates the camera; I can see it way, way down there. No living creature appears to be in current residence, so I decide to try to fish the thing out. I stick my arm into the hole, but my fingers grasp at empty air. I overextend a hiking pole, but that doesn't do the trick, either. I overextend my other pole, duct-tape the two together, end to end, and give that a whirl. Now I can reach the camera, but I still cannot succeed in moving it up the dirt walls of the hole. I become frustrated—I want my camera back! How else can I share this hike with my family, with Alex in particular?

Finally, I admit defeat and bid a very sad and fond farewell to my precious little camera, which, though I can plainly see, I simply cannot retrieve.

Now in a very bad mood and fully adorned with dirt, leaves, and spiderwebs, I continue my hike and quickly reach the intersection with Castle Trail. I climb up and over each of the Castles (large, tall outcrops of rocks that look like . . . well, castles) and witness breathtaking views into Castle Ravine. I would be filled with awe if I weren't too busy being distressed about my inability to take pictures.

After much steep hiking and a fair bit of rock scrambling, I arrive at the summit of Mount Jefferson. Gray clouds hang over my head, but the views into the valley are clear. It's a pretty sight, I guess. Somehow it's not as beautiful as it was when I was here before, with Alex.

Cold drops of rain begin to fall, so I don't spend much time lounging about. Down the Caps Ridge Trail I go, carefully stepping my way over the massive, inconvenient rocks. The drizzle is short-lived, lasting only a half hour at best. I am still a few hundred yards above tree line when the sun reclaims the sky.

What follows is the appearance of the most stunningly beautiful vision I have ever seen. To my right, just over there, almost so close I can touch it, is a rainbow so bright and clear that it seems as though my girls have drawn it with their oil pastels. There is a second, much fainter rainbow above the main one. They are both beneath me, the top of the second one just level with my eyes. The two rainbows stretch down and straddle the west side of Mount Jefferson, one pair of ends disappearing into the immediate trees below and the other pair reaching into Castle Ravine. It is a spectacular sight, and it takes my breath away. However, there is one thing missing, one thing that would perfect this experience. Alex. She would think this sight fantastic. I wish she were here.

Later, when I attempt to share my day with her, Alex gives me royal five-year-old attitude. Though at first she was okay with the idea of my hiking without her, now, after the fact, she is not. She asks if we can ascend something tomorrow. We can't, since our family already has plans. Alex doesn't speak to me again until the next morning, and even then she remains a bit of a sourpuss.

I tolerate her anger with good humor, for I feel it's a good sign. She's upset because she didn't go with me. This confirms that she's hiking all of these mountains because she wants to, and not because she's trying to please me. I don't want her to hike for me. I do love her company, yes, of course—but she has to want to be out there; that desire has to come from within, and she needs to know that I'm okay going by myself should she ever decide she doesn't want to do this anymore.

Luckily for me, Alex never wants to stop. However, every once in a while she does decide to take a two- or three-week break. During those times, I satisfy my own hiking urges by repeating peaks solo, even though the mountains aren't nearly as beautiful without her in them.

Some Risks Are Worth Taking

Winter 2008–2009

Winter approaches, and I worry how Alex will keep herself content during our assumed four- or five-month hiatus. Will she go stir-crazy if she doesn't get out there on a regular basis? As the fall weeks tick by, a seed of thought takes root in my head. Does Alex really need to stay home? Can we hike right through the seasons? Is it possible for a child to hike a 4K during winter?

Though I have no winter hiking experience, my gut feeling is yes, if Alex wants to learn how to winter hike, then she can. We can do this together. I need to talk to people, learn from them, figure out a few things, but sure we can. Where there's a will, there's a way.

Hugh did a lot of winter hiking and camping as a child, so I direct my first questions to him. With his guidance, I buy a winter sleeping bag and a sturdier bivy sack, both of which are roomy enough to hold

Alex and me in an emergency situation. Should Alex and I become stranded overnight, the use of these two items will keep us comfortably warm and dry, even if the temperatures plummet to thirty degrees below zero.

The next stop in my search for practical information is, of course, the Internet hiking forums. Unfortunately, as soon as I let on that I am thinking of taking Alex up the 4Ks during winter, I receive a good share of flak. Though some hikers are supportive, especially those who have met us, others are skeptical and point-blank call me insane. I don't blame them. I keep forgetting that most five-year-old children aren't climbing mountains at all, let alone during the coldest months of the year. I take the virtual hits but persevere. I know there is potential danger in this venture, however, I see no reason why we shouldn't try. If we're prepared, if I'm carrying all the things necessary to spend an unintentional night out, and—most important—if I don't mind turning back at any time for any reason, then why not give it a go and see what happens?

Our refusal to sit out winter ends up costing a pretty penny. Hugh insists that we not skimp on the gear, so I end up purchasing high-quality (and expensive!) items. The winter sleeping bag costs $800, the sturdier bivy sack costs $300. I buy dozens of chemical hand and body warmers, small packs that emit heat once exposed to oxygen, for a buck or two apiece. Winter boots, the kind that keep toes warm in subzero temperatures,

are $85 for Alex and $180 for me. Microspikes, little
sharp points that attach to the bottom of your boots
and make it possible to walk up slick trails without
slipping, are $50 a pair. More base layers, fleece gar-
ments, and heavy woolen socks are purchased. Wind
and rainproof pants and jackets, goggles (for snow
glare and prevention of frostbite around the eyes),
balaclavas, face masks, hats, windproof gloves, woolen
gloves (worn under the heavier, windproof ones), more
plastic whistles, snowshoes, insulated carriers for liquid (so our drinking water doesn't freeze), a large foam
mat—all these things need to be bought, and carried!
A bigger (and heavier) backpack in which to put all
this stuff is also purchased. The final thing I buy is an
updated personal locator beacon (PLB) for $650. This

handheld device, approximately the size and weight of an early 1990s cellular phone, will alert search and rescue personnel across the country of our exact global positioning system (GPS) location within three minutes of our pressing an SOS button. The grand total of our winter-prep purchases is between three and four thousand dollars. I justify the expense by telling myself (and Hugh) that even if Alex decides not to winter hike, we can use almost everything right outside in our backyard. Instead of hours on the trails, we'll spend hours building snow forts, no matter what the weather. We could winter camp a dozen feet from our front door.

It's not enough to simply buy the gear, of course. We each have to know how to use it. Alex and I spend a few hours setting up the bivy and placing our mat and sleeping bag inside of it. I show my daughter the new PLB and teach her how to push the right button. Hugh and I sit Alex down and explain how she is to keep herself warm, hydrated, and fed in the extremely unlikely event that I am somehow rendered unconscious. We stress that this will probably never happen, but that she must know what to do anyway, just in case. We emphasize that it sometimes takes search and rescue an entire night and day to find a lost hiker. We have her set up everything by herself, over and over again, until both Hugh and I are confident that she completely understands what she is to do. These drills are less morbid than they sound—we are only preparing our daughter for the worst kind of scenario, just as parents tell their

kids what to do in the event of a fire. It's precautionary, all of it. Alex knows this and therefore does not
become frightened.

We've now got the gear and as much knowledge as
can be had without firsthand experience. We're ready
to give this winter hiking thing a whirl.

November rolls around, the temperatures drop, and
half a foot of snow falls the day before a planned ascent of 4,302-foot Mount Willey. To my great surprise,
MadRiver, the "child hater" we met a couple of months
ago on the family hike up Mount Cardigan, sends me a
late-night private message through the hiking forums
and asks if he can accompany us the next morning.
He'd like to start later in the morning and catch up
to us on the trail. I tell him sure, of course, but please
understand if we hike at a much slower pace than what
he's used to. He assures me that a relaxed ascent won't
be a problem. I go to bed apprehensive about hiking
with a man with a reputation for hating children, but
excited for the new challenge that lies ahead.

And a challenge it most certainly is! Though it is
still technically fall and not yet winter, the temperatures are so low I fear my daughter will become immediately chilled in the frigid morning air; we begin the
hike dressed in all of our layers. We find it a struggle to
accommodate our clothing; it's quite difficult to walk

wearing so much bulk. Our face masks feel awkward, and Alex has difficulty breathing because she keeps getting black woolen bits of fuzz up her nose. She finds she can't use her hiking poles because she can't grip them while wearing her heavy gloves. If she takes her hands out of those gloves for even a second, her fingers become painfully cold.

We struggle up the steep initial couple tenths of a mile of the Ethan Pond Trail . . . and then something odd happens. I start to feel hot. I look down at Alex, who breathes heavily underneath her face mask. I bring her to a halt and remove the fleece from her nose and mouth. Her skin is red and damp. A moment ago she was chilled, but now she is sweating.

In the time it takes us to remove a few layers of clothes, we become chilled again. I decide to keep the layers off and see what happens. Alex and I resume our former pace up the slope, and as we go, I realize that the trick is to dress lightly and move quickly. If we wear too much, we'll overheat while ascending. If we wear too little and slow our pace or stop for even a moment, we'll become chilled. It takes a solid hour and many starts and stops to figure out exactly how much clothing each of us should wear in order to stay consistently comfortable for the longest amount of time. Alex becomes frustrated with having to go through this learning curve. She's used to everything being relatively easy. To stop, start, and stop again, to wear four layers of clothing, then two, then three, then one, then back to four . . . it's aggravating. I ask her many times if she wants to turn back, but she continually responds by saying, "We're here, let's do this."

MadRiver appears just as we reach the Willey Range Trail, about 1.6 miles into our hike. He ascends with strong and steady steps, his kilt fluttering in the frigid breeze. Alex throws herself onto the ground and lies in the snow as he approaches, weary and frustrated. MadRiver reaches us, looks down, and gives my daughter a wave. As I give him a hello hug, I murmur in his ear, "We may end up turning back—Alex is not exactly loving this." "No problem," he quietly answers.

I take a picture of the two of them: MadRiver standing over Alex by the trail sign, looking as though he's just killed her as she lies motionless in the snow. As I put away my camera, I hear her pick herself up and brush herself off. She offers a polite greeting before continuing up the trail.

It is an extremely difficult hike. The trail is unrelentingly steep, and there's not enough snow cover to completely fill in the gaps and gnarls in the root systems. Often we put our boots down on what we think is solid snow only to sink ankle-deep into a lightly covered chasm. This awkward footing, combined with the precipitous grade of the trail and our continual on-again, off-again clothing ritual, makes for a very onerous morning. Alex stomps her way up the mountain, constantly muttering at all the obstacles. MadRiver is amused at her fury and impressed by her determination. Though I too admire my daughter's tenacity, I realize that if MadRiver weren't with us, I'd have turned us around by now. This hike is taking much longer than I had originally planned; there are so many new things to deal with, and it is extremely cold out here! However, MadRiver *is* with us, and he has a fair bit of winter hiking experience under his belt. Each of us is warm, fed, and hydrated, and both MadRiver and I have enough gear to, as he puts it, "take care of a troop of Girl Scouts." I feel safe continuing onward and upward.

We do eventually make it all 2.7 miles to the top, though it takes us five hours to do so. Reaching the summit chases away some of Alex's blues, and as we stand at a viewpoint and look down onto massive Webster Cliff, my daughter's face allows a smile to creep onto her features. Webster Cliff is one wide, scratched-up surface of rock that towers over the valley below. In today's bright morning, its frosty boulders sparkle in the sunlight. It's a scene my younger daughter, Sage, would love. There's fairy dust in mass quantities over there, shimmering happily, celebrating life's hard-earned pleasures.

Our descent is a completely different experience from our tedious morning climb. Going down is so much easier than coming up! The three of us chat amicably. MadRiver does not speak down to my daughter; he neither uses a high-pitched voice nor insults her intelligence. Instead, he converses as one would with an adult. My esteem for him, which has already risen with every patient step he has taken, rises into the stratosphere. He asks Alex about the hikes she has already done, the kinds of things she likes to do, and how she gets along with her sister. Alex answers all his questions, then asks some of her own. Does he have children (no), is he married (yes), where does he live (close to us), and how many mountains has he hiked (too many to count). As I listen to the two of them banter back and forth, I can't help but wonder what prompted the woman at Mount Cardigan to warn me about this fellow. Though a strange sight with his grizzled gray hair and ever-fluttering kilt, he has been nothing but kind to us. Not many adults would willingly walk so slowly on a winter hike with a child who wasn't their own son or daughter.

We reach a flat section of trail, and Alex skips ahead, her energy surging as it always does during a descent. When I think she is out of earshot, I gather my courage and say, "You know, I heard that you weren't that fond of children."

MadRiver smiles and answers, "I'm not. I don't like whining, I don't like screaming, and I don't like misbehaving brats. But Alex doesn't whine, she doesn't scream, and she's definitely not a brat. Actually, I don't think she's really a child. She's a twenty-year-old hiker trapped in a very small person's body."

Okay. I can roll with that.

A couple of snowy weeks later, Alex tells me she's ready to give another winter mountain a go. This surprises me, since she was so miserable during our ascent of Mount Willey. I take her at her word, though, and search the Internet for recent 4K trip reports. It doesn't take me long to find a post regarding a trail that has been recently traveled and "packed out." Since many people hike the 4Ks, even during winter, snowshoe paths along the usual routes are quickly established, even after a heavy snowstorm. The footing, therefore, becomes extremely easy if the snowpack is deep; this we first discover as we climb 4,802-foot Mount Moosilauke using the Glencliff Trail on a brisk December day. The ascent is a piece of cake. It feels like we're walking on a smooth (albeit steep) white sidewalk, and, unlike our experience on Mount Willey, there are no exposed rocks or roots for us to trip over. Even our clothing becomes less of a hassle as we get used to the frequent putting on and removal of layers.

Alex and I move up the mountain in very good spirits. I continually hand my daughter an insulated bottle of hot chocolate, from which she drinks in hefty gulps. This liquid refreshment keeps her both hydrated and energized, and she bounds up the trail an extremely happy camper. It is a joyous morning, and Alex frequently comments on the splendor of the winter wonderland through which we travel. Each branch of evergreen holds a little pile of snow; every tree trunk is coated with sparkling ice. It's as though Hollywood were here before us this morning, creating the perfect scene for its next Christmas blockbuster.

Everything goes well—so well that I almost feel we have this winter thing under total control—until we reach the intersection with the Moosilauke Carriage Road. This intersection is close to tree line, and we now begin to hear the wind whipping around the mountain. Every few seconds, a renegade gust blasts its way through a branchy gap and shoves itself in our faces. It is an extremely unpleasant feeling at best, for that wind is mean; it's nasty. It bites at our cheeks and makes us wince. We drop our packs and hastily don all layers of clothing, starting with headwear. I make certain that every inch of Alex's skin is covered, as it won't take more than a few minutes for her skin to succumb to frostbite if that wind remains so brazen. I take special care with her face, adjusting her goggles so they overlap her face mask, tightening the straps so that her head movements can't shift the material. Once we're above tree line, it will be difficult, if not impossible, for me to make certain none of her skin is exposed at any time. Most of my focus will be in keeping the two of us upright.

I am so consumed with making sure her precious face and head are protected that I forget to pay attention to the rest of her body. As a result, when we step out of the trees to begin the final push toward the summit, just a few tenths of a mile from the peak, Alex is not wearing her windproof gloves. She does wear two layers of woolen mittens, but these do nothing to protect her fingers from the wind. Without that outer layer, the thin skin on her digits can feel every icy and unmerciful blast.

I do not immediately realize my mistake. The wind roars with indignation at our bold approach and does its best to push us over. I grab Alex's arm and practically drag her up the slope in an effort to keep her on her feet. She yells something at me, but I can't make out her words. A wall of air slams into us, and we both fall off the path. Alex tumbles into a nearby cairn, and I dive after her, momentarily worried that she will blow off the mountain.

"Are you okay?" I holler. I try to read Alex's emotions, but the task is impossible; her facial expressions are hidden beneath her face mask and balaclava.

"My hands hurt!" she yells.

I look down and finally realize what Alex is missing.

"Mama, they really hurt!" Alex's shout is tinged with panic, and I realize my daughter is frightened and in pain. That's that. This ascent is over.

We're now perhaps two hundred yards from the

summit, an easy five- or ten-minute walk if the wind weren't behaving in such a contrary manner. I know full well we're going to abort, but I want to give Alex the courtesy of making the decision herself.

"We're very close to the summit now. Are you okay to continue, or do you want to turn back?" I ask, prepared to exercise my veto power should she make the wrong choice.

Alex hesitates for a literal second, then answers, "Turn back!"

Excellent. My daughter has good sense.

Without another word, I pull Alex to a standing position and lead her back down the trail, battling the confrontational wind every step of the way. As soon as we are back in the protection of the trees, I get to work on her hands. I remove her gloves and put her bare skin on my stomach, underneath my four layers of clothing.

"Are you okay?" I speak in a normal tone as the wind no longer whips about our ears.

"Yes," Alex answers. She removes one of her hands from my stomach long enough to yank off her face mask. "I didn't like that wind—it really hurt my fingers."

"How are they now? Are they warming up a bit?"

"Yeah."

Her face clouds as she stands there, hands on my stomach, goggles askew.

"We didn't make it to the top, Mama." The words

come slowly, as though she's giving me some unexpected and unfortunate news.

"I know, honey."

"Is that okay?"

I smile. "Would you rather we went all the way up but lost a few of these fingers?" I take out her hands and kiss the fingers in question.

She answers in the form of a lopsided smile. I hand over her three layers of gloves.

"Do you want to try again? Now, I mean."

Alex slowly shakes her head.

"Good!" I exclaim. Her eyebrows rise. "I'm proud of you, kid. You just became a real hiker. Real hikers know when to continue and when to turn back."

"Even when they're really close to the summit?"

"Especially when they're really close to the summit. Better to turn back ten feet from the summit than to reach the peak but not make it back to the car. How are your hands?"

Alex smiles broadly and declares her fingers toasty. Her expression seems satisfied, proud even. She *should* feel proud. She just exhibited good, sound judgment, and she doesn't seem all that upset at having to turn back. It's important for her not to become too disappointed if she doesn't reach the top. Her mind should always be on safety first and the summit second.

We make our way down the Carriage Road feeling rather good about ourselves, Alex humming a random tune and me congratulating myself on a successful winter hike. Who cares if we didn't reach the summit? We're both safe and having a good time.

At the top of Glencliff Trail, Alex is struck by a brilliant idea. More than two and a half snowy miles of downhill trail lie at our feet. How can we not take advantage? She sits, a mad gleam in her eye, and announces her intention to "butt slide all the way back to the car."

And that's exactly what we do. We laugh and shout and fly down the mountain, my giggles sounding every bit as childlike as Alex's. Down the packed trail we go, at a clip fast enough to provoke involuntary hoots of glee. When necessary, I act as a human brake for my daughter; she laughingly slams into my back whenever I slow our descent. The two of us behave in the silliest fashion, and by the time we reach the car, we are thoroughly convinced that winter hiking is more fun than, well, anything.

Alex and I summit six peaks during the official calendar winter season. In doing so, we discover that the joys of winter hiking far outweigh the inconveniences. Heavier packs and colder air are happily managed; such things are a small price to pay for the sight of snow-capped summits and icicled trees, the ease of snow sidewalks, the feel of crisp mountain air, and the joy of fast and furious "butt sliding."

We are never again forced to turn back. Much of that probably has to do with the fact that I become very picky over which days we venture out. On extremely chilly days (subzero in the valley), we stay home. On days with considerable snow in the forecast, we stay home. On days where the following nights are supposed to be considerably cold, or considerably snowy, we stay home. I also keep us below tree line, as I know, from our Moosilauke experience, that the number of potential problems increases exponentially once you step into the windy and barren alpine zone.

As the weeks go on and my trip reports are posted, my Internet critics silence themselves, and our informal approval ratings soar. Several people write and tell me that they had been worried when they found out I was taking Alex up the 4Ks in the winter, but now that they've read my blog, they can see how prepared and levelheaded I am. Though I'm not usually one to care what other people think, these messages buoy me. I can't help but feel good about receiving the support of my hiking peers, and it can't hurt Alex to have people thinking favorable thoughts about her.

Though Alex and I enjoy winter hiking, we are ready for the reappearance of rocks and sunshine when the season eventually draws to a close. Spring arrives, bringing with it warmer temperatures and longer days. As pleasant as spring may be in the valley, however, we soon discover it's a horrible season for hiking.

To Get to Where She Wants to Go, a Girl Must Punch Through Rotting Snow

Peak #30: Mount Moriah, April 25, 2009

Springtime in the Whites brings the return of many natural treasures: abundant sunshine, warmer temperatures, the reappearance of rocks and leaves, the sounds of birds, and the tracks of bear. Springtime also means a lighter burden on the shoulders, as the heavy winter sleeping bag can be switched out of the backpack for a lighter three-season one, and the emergency camping stove can be replaced with an ultralight box of weatherproof matches. In addition, it's no longer necessary to carry a multitude of water bottles. The frozen brooks are melting; water can be collected and purified with iodine tablets wherever there's a stream crossing.

These are the positive aspects of the advent of spring. There is, however, one negative aspect. One nasty, ornery, pain-in-the-rear aspect: snow.

Snow during winter is delightful. It's solid beneath

your feet, and it stays in place. If you're wearing snow-shoes, you can float on top of it, and there will be little to no inconvenient sinks as you make your way up and over a mountain.

Snow during springtime is, simply put, awful. It's not the nice white fluffy stuff. It's old, it's weak, and it's rotting. One second you're walking on a firm side-walk, the next you're dropping through slush, even with your once-trusty snowshoes strapped to your feet. Much of the time, in spite of your best efforts and psychological preparations, you sink to your thighs with every other step. It's maddening.

Such are the words of warning given to me from well-meaning hikers upon my announcement that Alex and I will hike straight through the spring. I take these folks seriously, and I also remember the failed Tecumseh attempt the year before, when I had both girls with me, and I hadn't a clue yet as to what I was doing. However, Alex and I now have twenty-nine peaks under our belts, and we feel adequately prepared and experienced to take on this challenge. And honestly, Alex and I cannot fathom taking a four- to six-week break from hiking. We figure we'll just take it slowly and adjust to the unstable hiking surface. We managed winter; we should be able to manage spring.

The day starts out well enough. The snow has completely melted from the lower portion of the Stony Brook Trail, and we ascend the first leg of 4,049-foot

Mount Moriah feeling warm and fine. Free of our winter fleece and base layers, both of us sport shorts and synthetic T-shirts. We feel good. We feel *light*.

The first mile is an easy jaunt toward Stony Brook. We cross the water without much ado, the soles of our boots barely touching the water as we skip across the stepping stones. I mark where we cross well, for this brook will probably look very different when we return later in the day. The sun will melt the snow throughout the afternoon, and the excess water will pour down the mountain, swelling all the streams and rivulets. It may be necessary to get our boots and legs wet on the way out, or I may choose to camp if the water appears too deep to cross. No worries: I have all necessary gear, and my cell phone works on this section of trail, so I can contact Hugh if the need arises.

Onward we trek. The trail turns upward. And there lies the snow.

Initially, it's not so bad. Rocks poke their heads above the sea of glistening white, and Alex enjoys hopping from stone to stone. It's an amusing novelty, wearing shorts under a bright sun while stepping over winter's leftovers. However, soon the snow covers the path completely, and it's necessary to step directly onto—or, should I say, *into*—the cold and wet stuff.

Alex makes her way through the next few tenths of a mile by walking in the middle of the trail where it's firmer, packed down from last winter's many snow-shoes. I, being much heavier than my daughter, sink constantly no matter where I step.

It doesn't take long before the snow situation worsens. With each foot of elevation gain, the snow becomes softer and deeper. I don my snowshoes in an attempt to make life easier for myself, but the effort is in vain. I continue to sink repeatedly, making giant snowshoe-size holes in the melting snowpack.

Alex continues to have a better time of it. As long as she keeps to the center of the trail, she is usually able to stay on top of the mess. Her face doesn't look all that happy, though. I chalk it up to the rotting snow.

We keep at it for two miles before deciding to take a snack break. The dry top of a medium-size boulder provides a convenient island on which to sit. Finally, something pleasant! For the first time in months, we're able to sit without immediately becoming chilled. My sports watch informs me of the temperature; it's a seasonal sixty-five degrees.

Twenty minutes go by in silence. Had this been months ago, when Alex and I were first starting out, I would have worried about her quiet demeanor and peppered her with questions. Now she is seasoned enough to tell me what she needs, and I no longer have to nag her about drinking enough, eating enough, or wearing the proper amount of clothing. I concentrate on my peanuts and choose not to interrupt her thoughts.

Alex eventually puts down her bag of trail mix,

looks at me, and pulls the lid off a big can of troubling discussion.

"Jacob told me I can't be good at math because I'm a girl." Alex shoves her foot down into the snow and then yanks it back up, splattering little bits of pebbly white granules everywhere.

Crap. I knew I'd have to have this kind of talk with her at some point during her young life, but I was hoping it would at least wait until her age hit the double digits.

"That doesn't make any sense," I say. "You're two grade levels ahead of him in math."

"He also said that I can't build things very well . . . because I'm a girl." Alex scowls at a nearby tree as she speaks. I can see the color rising in her cheeks as her temper threatens to get the best of her.

Great. Thanks, Jacob. Guess I'll be having a discussion with his mother as soon as we return to Somerville.

Jacob's mother actually does a fine job with her son, and she is not one to tolerate sexist language. These comments likely reflect a new influence on Jacob, a boy who recently moved into the neighborhood. Alex met this kid once, when he had come over to Jacob's house to see if Jacob wanted to play. Upon seeing Alex, the charming lad had sniffed, "I don't like girls," turned on his heels, and stalked off. Alex had been understandably hurt and confused by his behavior. She had never experienced gender discrimination before.

Jacob probably now sees this boy on a regular basis, as I assume these recent comments reflect a burgeoning friendship. At least I know that as soon as I speak with Jacob's mother, Jacob will be set straight, and Alex will never again hear such comments come out of her friend's mouth.

Unhappy thoughts are swirling through my head as my strong and beautiful daughter, who just turned six a couple of months ago, sits there kicking the snow around and waiting for me to respond. My little Amazon, who hikes New Hampshire's highest mountains with great stamina and joy. My Alex, who would probably leave both Jacob and his new neighbor in the dust should they ever attempt to climb a mountain of any height.

"Do you think what he was saying was true?" I finally answer, after calming myself.

"No!" comes the immediate response, accompanied by a scowl so deep it threatens to swallow her face.

"Then why do you think he said that?"

"I don't know!" Alex is frustrated and obviously looking to me for concrete answers. I wish I could give them to her. All I can do is explain that there are many people who believe that girls are not as good as boys. I don't want to do this; I don't want this belief to be out there; I don't want my innocent daughter to have to deal with all that bull. But I can't shield her forever.

"There are some boys who think that girls can't do things just because they're girls," I begin.

"Well *that's* stupid," Alex says.

We've been sitting for a while now, and I am beginning to be mindful of the time. I pull Alex to her feet, and we continue our ascent.

As we fight through the rotting snow, I give Alex a brief history of the American woman. Our status as property, our role as child bearers, our lack of the right to vote. The relatively recent changes to the law that finally afforded us civil rights. The present problem of women not making as much money as men for doing the same job, the lack of extended maternity leave. I repeatedly step, sink, and yank my foot free of the snow's grip as our discussion expands to the topic of women in certain other countries. Women hurt and killed for speaking their mind. Teenage girls married off unwillingly. Though my explanations are mere sketches of very basic information, I feel I paint an accurate overall picture. Alex listens intently, her fury pushing her forward. Her disgust at the unfairness of it all is taken out on the snow. Step, sink, yank, kick.

We are close to a minor stream crossing when I step on what appears to be solid snow and immediately sink up to my waist. "Fudge!" I loudly exclaim. Except I don't say "Fudge." Alex's eyes grow wide and round, and she smiles for the first time since leaving the car.

I slowly pull myself out of the hole my body has created, take another snowshoe step, and promptly sink once again.

My daughter stays on top of the ground during this section. She is lighter, and the snow underneath her feet does not crumble. I keep stepping on surfaces I think are solid, only to have the snow give way beneath me. As I repeatedly drag my body up and over, I hope that throughout her life, Alex's footing is as good off the trail as it is on. I hope she looks where she steps and judges correctly. I hope she puts herself in social situations where her environment is as it seems to be, free from the land mines of sexism. I hope she learns how to navigate the world so that she can get to where she wants to go, with as little sinking into unnecessary mush as possible.

This especially nasty section blessedly ends just before we reach the intersection with the Carter-Moriah Trail. We sit at the trail sign, recharging our bodies and resting our legs. Alex looks at me with her sky-blue eyes and asks, "What am I supposed to do when a boy tells me I'm not good enough?"

Oh, I wish I could give her some magic words. Words she could say to such people, words that would melt their preconceived notions like the warm sunshine melts the snow from the mountains. Alas, it is not that simple.

"Alex, my dear daughter, all you can do is be

yourself. Never hide your strengths. Do exactly what you want to do, even if someone tells you that girls aren't supposed to do such things. Those statements—those words Jacob said—they're lies. Lies told by foolish people who are, for some reason, afraid of a woman's strength."

Alex's brow furrows as she chews some walnuts. Then she asks another question I had hoped I wouldn't have to field until she was much older. "Why don't you work outside the home?"

Ah, here it is. Why *don't* I work outside the home? Me, with my master's degree from Harvard University? Me, the fiercely independent woman who has traveled the country and the world? Me, the woman who once had high dreams of great academic achievement? Me, who sometimes worries how a stay-at-home mother can be a strong, shining example to her daughters?

The answer is simple: I don't work outside the home because for the moment I am too busy working *inside* the home. I tell Alex this, but my answer isn't good enough for her.

"Does this mean that mothers can't be scientists or doctors or anything else?"

"No, honey, that's not it. Of course they can. However, once you have children, you need to focus on them. For some families, this means the mother puts her own career aside for a while. In other families, the father is the one to stay home while the mother goes out to work. Or both parents take turns staying with the kids. Or the grandparents come and help out. Or you hire a good nanny, and you come home as soon and as often as you can. Or you work from home. There are many options to choose from nowadays."

Alex is silent for a while as we move closer toward the summit. We reach a series of snow-free ledges, and a stunning view leaps out at us. Mount Washington and its Presidential Range neighbors loom nearby, their tall, snowy peaks glistening in the sun. They're beautiful, majestic. Alex stands tall and holds her hiking stick high above her head, a huge smile on her face as we are reminded of today's purpose, of our immediate destiny. Mount Moriah's peak is not so far away. The worst appears to be over. If we can just persevere for a little while longer, then we'll stand on our goal, victorious. The views from right here and now are gorgeous. They'll only get better.

We move along the ledges, then back into the trees for a while, then out among some sharp and rocky outcroppings.

"Mama, do you miss it? Do you miss working away from home?"

"No," I immediately say. It's almost the truth. Most of the time, I don't miss it. I don't miss office politics, or measuring my worth by the status of my career, or fretting over runs in my pantyhose.

However, I do, at times, miss pursuing my own

career. There are little things too, things my pre-children self took for granted. Having an uninterrupted coffee break. Privacy in the bathroom. Riding an elevator without having to tell someone to quit jumping up and down.

We come to a spur path that climbs a short and

steep distance to Moriah's summit. Finally. Almost there. I turn and start upward, but Alex keeps her feet planted at the intersection.

"Why not? Why don't you miss it?"

Such questions today!

Sighing, I step back, drop to my knees, and look her in the eyes.

"Alex, I lived on my own for fourteen years before having you and Sage. In those fourteen years, I worked outside the home. I also traveled across the United States and visited many other countries. I did all kinds of things with my life. But you know what?"

"What?"

"Being with you and Sage—*that* is the most exciting thing I've ever done. Raising you, listening to you, reading to you, loving you, being there for you—there is nothing I could ever do that is more interesting or more important than that. If I left you and Sage to work outside the home, I would die of boredom."

I hug her, but Alex does not remain in the embrace for more than a moment. She draws back and asks yet another question.

"Other mothers work outside the home. Are they wrong?"

"I can't know what's best for other mothers and their children, Alex. I know only what's best for me, and for the two of you."

Alex turns and walks up the last few dozen yards to Moriah's highest point. We unbuckle our packs and sit on a bare rock, happy to be at the peak. I am sore and exhausted.

Alex smiles and surveys the view with pride. I don't need to tell her that this was a difficult hike. She knows it was; we're now past the point of my having to praise her for making it to the top. Out here on the trail, Alex is a woman-child. She has no use for pats on the head.

"What will you think of me if I work outside the home?" she asks.

"Alex, I want you to have whatever career you want to have. It's not my place to tell you how to manage everything. You'll have to figure it out on your own, with the help of your baby's father. Just know that if ever you want my help, I'll be there for you."

When we both feel adequately rested and well fed, we make our way down the mountain. Unfortunately, the descent is just as torturous as the ascent. The snow has softened even more in the day's bright sunshine, and I sink over and over again into the rotting slush. Even Alex, who had managed to stay on top most of the way up, now sinks to her waist repeatedly.

Our words are few during the afternoon hours. With every sink and fall, our legs scrape painfully against the topmost layer of snow. Alex's calves are bright red before we're even halfway down. I ask her if she'd like to change into long pants, but she says no.

My legs are holding up well until I manage to fall and wedge one of Alex's snowshoes into my knee. The shoe had fallen off my pack earlier, and I had chosen to carry it instead of fastening it back on. When I fall, I let go of the snowshoe, and it lands, cleats up, directly in front of me. Down goes my knee, straight into the shoe's sharp bits. Expletives leave my mouth as I stand, snowshoe embedded in my knee.

Alex's eyes grow wide at the sight, and I quickly wrench the thing from my flesh. There is blood, but not so much that Alex blanches. I tell her I'm fine, and we carry onward. I'm too tired to properly secure the thing to my pack, and I don't do anything to clean up my knee. The pain is minimal, and I want to keep moving.

Alex renews our earlier conversation.

"What should I do if the boys won't let me play?"

Crunch-swoosh! My legs punch through, sink, punch through, sink.

"It's up to you. You could play anyway and try to win them over. Or you could choose to walk away."

Crunch-swoosh! Alex's legs mimic mine.

"If I try to play with them, maybe they'll understand that they're wrong."

Crunch-swoosh!

"Maybe. Or maybe they'll choose to exclude you anyway."

Crunch-swoosh!

"Then how do I know what to do?"

Crunch-swoosh!

"It's not always clear. With kids, like these boys you're talking about, it's kind of difficult. They're just reflecting their parents' attitudes. They're confused. On one hand, they're trying to figure it all out for themselves, while on the other hand, they want to fit in with their friends and live up to their parents' expectations. With grown-ups, it's very different. If a man tells you that you're not allowed to do something because you're a woman, then you can have the government make him do the right thing. Grown men can lose their jobs or be made to pay a large fine if they don't allow women the same rights as men. Kids, though . . . it's up to the parents to teach them to do the right thing. Nothing much happens to boys who say sexist things to girls."

The snow thins and becomes less problematic. Our pace increases. Fifteen more minutes, and we're out of that mess and back onto dry trail. Thank God.

"Some boys are okay, right?" Alex asks, her back straight and her stride strong.

"Yes, definitely! Most of them are okay."

"What about men? Are most of them okay too?"

"Yes, most of them are okay. At least in this country. Make no mistake, though—you will indeed meet and have to deal with some bad ones. It's just part of life as a woman. Do your best to avoid the unfair ones when you can, but never let any of them stand in your way."

We reach the water crossing and are now one mile away from our car. This morning, Stony Brook was easily navigated. Now, however, the day's melted snow has found its way into the water and the level has risen to just below my knees. I'm confident we can get across, but our feet and lower legs will get soaked.

I tell Alex that we're going to wade across the part we crossed earlier, and she nods her head in agreement. Keeping a firm grip on Alex's upper arm, I lead us through the frigid water. The current pushes at our legs, and Alex stumbles, but my hold keeps her upright, and we reach the other side without mishap.

Calves and feet drenched, we stand, Mount Moriah checked off the list. Alex looks sturdy and victorious, her hands on her hips as she stares down the path before us. The afternoon is waning; sunset is only an hour away.

"I can do what I want with my life, right? I can get to where I want to go?"

"Yes, Alex. I've no doubt you'll be able to do anything you want to do. However, sometimes the path might be like the one up Mount Moriah in April. Sometimes you're going to have to punch through rotting snow to get to where you want to go. You might end up feeling tired and angry, but if you just keep at it, if you just keep moving forward and dealing with everything the best way you can, then you will indeed reach your goal."

"And if I have babies?"

"Then you'll make your own choices and do your best to figure it out."

I fear my words are inadequate, but this is the best I can do. I don't know how to better prepare her for the inevitable difficulties she will face as she makes her way through life.

The two of us step quickly down the trail, the distance between ourselves and our car narrowing every second, Alex looking full of heavy thought.

Roll with the Punches

Peak #36: Mount Isolation, June 27–28, 2009

The spruce grouse is not a ferocious species. There aren't any books advising what to do should you meet one on a trail, and there aren't any warnings about them on the New Hampshire Fish and Game website. No one worries about crossing paths with a grouse. While it's true that many are not afraid of humans, these calf-high birds present no threat. They may wait until you're within a few feet of them before they fly away, but they will indeed fly away.

Except, of course, for the grouse on the Rocky Branch Trail. This particular individual is a creature of legend, a bird of angry bravado that has been featured in many a peakbagger's trip report. I have read all about this fowl's aggressive nature and bold demeanor, and its ability to fly at grown men and send them screaming down the trail. I don't think this bird has ever succeeded in seriously injuring anyone, but everyone desperately wishes to avoid it nonetheless.

And now here it is, a few yards in front of me, pacing back and forth and hissing. Yes, hissing.

Alex and I are about four miles up 4,005-foot Mount Isolation, one of the more difficult and notorious 4Ks. Reaching this particular summit means hiking almost fifteen round-trip miles over slick, mud-covered rocks, wading through three potentially dangerous water crossings . . . and making our way through the territory of one reportedly bold and extremely grumpy grouse.

Thankfully, my daughter and I are not alone with this bird. LRiz, an amiable and enthusiastic young athlete, contacted me the night before and asked if she could join us, at least for part of the first day. She wanted to start the hike with us, then go ahead after a few miles and speedily complete the trip on her own. I gladly agreed to her company. This lovely twenty-one-year-old is incredibly fit; she's one of the few who can hike an entire range in one day, go to sleep, wake up, and hike another range the next day. Just as cheerful as she is strong, her presence always brightens the moment. Alex adores her; MadRiver is coming with us as well, and he is cherished and much appreciated, but LRiz is a young woman, and Alex enjoys the sisterhood vibe she receives from this positive female role model.

Alex and LRiz are behind me when the grouse steps out. MadRiver is not yet with us, as he preferred to start later in the morning and catch up to us on the trail.

"It's the grouse, it's the grouse!" I gasp, my words running together in surprise and fright. My hands reach for my camera, for I absolutely must document this encounter.

LRiz draws in a horrified breath. She's met this critter before, on a previous trip up Mount Isolation. When she sees what my hands are doing, she emphatically whispers, "Don't take its picture! That makes it really angry!" I look into her frightened face and realize she's not kidding. I leave my camera where it is.

"What is it?" Alex asks as she squeezes between LRiz and me, trying to get a better look.

"Just a bird, honey," I say, but my voice wavers.

The grouse has edged closer to us during our few seconds of commiseration while continuing to walk back and forth across the path. It keeps one red eye fixed on me while it bobs along, and its loud chatter informs me that it Is Not Afraid. It is telling me that it can beat the crap out of me if it really wants to. I believe it.

"What are we going to do?" Alex wants to know. Okay, time for me to mother up.

"Well, we have to keep going, right?" I try to sound brave, I really do, but that waver just won't leave my voice, and the expression on my daughter's face turns from curiosity to fear.

"Okay, just stay between LRiz and me," I direct her. "Let's all move together. Alex, you stay in the middle, and we'll casually walk past it. The worst it can do is peck at our boots, right?" I plaster a fake smile on my face, gather my courage, and take one step forward.

The grouse reacts instantly. Screaming in outrage, it quick-steps directly toward my leading foot.

I let out a small shriek and hurriedly retreat, running into Alex and pushing her against LRiz.

The grouse halts its charge and goes back to its former pacing, remaining much too close to my foot. Its red eye gleams with triumph.

LRiz takes a deep breath and does the bravest thing I can imagine under the circumstances. She volunteers to go first. I ask her if she's sure, and, after taking the proverbial gulp, she answers in the affirmative. Then, with a look of admirable determination, she steps boldly along the path toward the grouse.

Again, the grouse reacts instantly. This time, however, instead of striding toward an advancing boot, it leaps off the ground and makes a flying dash toward LRiz's chest. LRiz lets out a high-pitched cry of surprise, then manages to dodge the grouse and flee down the trail. The grouse rounds and attempts another attack, this time at LRiz's back. I follow close behind, shouting in a desperate attempt to distract the flying menace, keeping Alex close behind me all the while. Finally, the grouse drops back down to the ground and stalks away into the neighboring brush, looking highly satisfied.

Alex and I catch up to LRiz, and I ask if she's all right. I'm convinced there will be blood and peck marks all over her, but miraculously, she is fine. There are no holes in her pack or clothing, and she claims she didn't feel any contact. Apparently, it was all one big noisy bluff. I thank her profusely for taking the hit, and I apologize for not having the courage to go first myself. She's a very good sport about it.

Not five minutes later, we hear footsteps coming from behind. It's MadRiver.

"Did you see the grouse?" I ask, thinking he must have, since it so recently bullied us.

"No," he answers, with a twinkle in his eye. "But I know you ladies did, 'cause I heard the screams."

It's now an easy mile or so to where we will later spend the night. The only difficulty between here and the shelter is a twenty-foot-wide brook. The water is not so high as to present a danger, but it's a slight challenge to cross nonetheless. I am able to guide Alex to the other side by leading her across the tallest rocks. Her boots get wet, but her feet do not. No big deal.

This time around, anyway.

We take a quick break at the three-sided wooden structure that will later serve as our sleeping quarters. MadRiver stashes half the contents of his pack in one of the corners and unrolls a mat diagonally across the floor. Our informal reservations now made, we pull the straps of our packs back over our shoulders and stand, ready to continue onward. My back does not want to straighten all the way and the muscles on either side of my spine spasm sharply. I briefly consider taking out half my gear and leaving it alongside MadRiver's belongings in the corner. I let the thought pass, however, as I don't want to risk not having something I might need. What if I fall and break my leg a mile from the shelter? What if the temperatures drop unexpectedly? What if we are forced to spend the night near the summit for some unforeseeable reason? The weight of the what-ifs is much heavier than the weight of my pack. Better to keep the tent and sleeping bags with me, for I'd much rather deal with the backache than the constant worry.

Two more miles behind us. That's almost six since we left the car. The summit is now a mile and a half away. Of course, after we tag it, we'll have to turn around and hike all the way back down to the shelter. My legs ache, and I feel an intense urge to whine. Alex's legs must be about to fall off; I don't know how she manages to keep going. I stare at her back as she tromps up the trail ahead of me. Her body looks strong; she looks capable. She has to be tired, though. Perhaps I should call for a break. We do, after all, have headlamps with us. Is it really necessary to make it back to the shelter before nightfall?

Rummmble. The distant sound wipes the musings from my mind, and my daughter comes to a sudden halt. MadRiver and LRiz stop moving as well, and for a moment I hear nothing but my own heavy panting.

RUMMMBLE. I take a step toward Alex, and she turns to me wide eyed, her lips tightly pressed together. *Yes,* I tell her with my gaze, *that is what you think it is.* Her complexion fades to a spectral shade of alabaster.

The air around us suddenly changes. A cold wind pushes away the summer's heat and forces its way around us. Shivering, I look up and watch the last of the blue fade from the angry sky.

MadRiver drops his pack and tears open the top compartment. A few seconds later, a large plastic tarp and a few bungee cords lie at my feet. "It won't help if there's lightning, but at least we'll stay dry," he mutters as his eyes survey the neighboring trees.

The wind picks up. The rain is coming soon, so we have to hurry. LRiz and I help MadRiver attach the bungee cords to the sides of the plastic. We then stretch the material over our heads and fasten the other ends of the cords to trees. The result is a roof just large enough to shelter the four of us and our packs. We huddle together and wait for the inevitable downpour.

BOOM!

The rain arrives all at once. The heavy drops bounce off our plastic roof and splatter onto the dirt below.

LRiz asks Alex how she's doing. Alex answers, "Fine." Her voice is faint and unconvincing.

Thankfully, the storm moves away as quickly as it came, departing only five minutes after its arrival. Grateful for the lack of hailstones and the presence of two other adults, I help MadRiver fold the tarp and retrieve his bungees. Alex stands off to the side, looking relieved and a little surprised. I ask her what she's thinking. She tells me that this thunderstorm wasn't very scary.

"Not all of them are like the one on Mount Tom," I tell her.

"Good to know," she replies.

Just one more mile stands between us and the summit. One long, miserable mile. The recent brief but heavy downpour has turned this trail into a fast-running stream, and I slosh through ankle-high water as I unhappily push myself toward the top of this blasted mountain. The water is calf-high to Alex. My daughter valiantly splashes onward, a little bundle of can-do attitude in the midst of three tired and cranky adults.

LRiz suddenly bids adieu and picks up her pace. It's time for her to move at her natural speed, which is light-years faster than ours. She wants to get back to her car before nightfall. I envy her. She'll probably be warm and dry in her home before we've made it back down to the shelter. I watch as she quickly disappears up the trail.

An outrageously short amount of time later, LRiz reappears. She's touched the summit cairn already! "It's beautiful up there!" she yells as she flies by. The three of us stare after her for a second, then turn our weary bodies to resume our slow trudge.

Maybe it is actually beautiful up here. I've no idea. I don't think Alex does, either. We're at the top, and the skies are mostly clear, and we can see out and down into the valley. There's even a rainbow arching over half the landscape. I suppose if we weren't completely worn out, we would think of all this as pretty. I look at Alex, sitting by the cairn and staring dully into the distance. My daughter has not complained once on this hike, but she must be tired. I'm tired. I'm more than tired. I'm ready to forgo the shelter and curl up right next to the pile of rocks at my feet.

"Hey, Alex," I say.

"What?" she answers. Ah, there it is—the fatigue is evident in her voice. She sounds exhausted. No problem. I have our tent, I have our sleeping bags. If she can't make it to the shelter, then we'll just sleep close to here.

"How'd you like that grouse?"

Alex pauses briefly before giving her answer. "I didn't."

"What about the thunder?"

"Nope."

"How about the rain? Did you like the rain?"

A hint of a smile plays at the left corner of her mouth.

"Uh, no."

"How about that river-trail we sloshed through? You must have loved that."

Some of the twinkle comes back into my daughter's eyes. "Still no," she answers.

"Now for a serious question. Are you too tired to make it back to the shelter? We can sleep near here if you like. That's not a problem."

Alex turns her face away from mine and gazes back out at the landscape. The rainbow has brightened a bit. Its red stripe is particularly bold, and it overshadows the rest of the spectrum.

"I'm okay," Alex says after a few minutes.

MadRiver calls to us from a dozen yards away. He is ready to head down. Alex and I struggle to our feet and follow him.

We make it to the shelter a few hours later, feet soaked, legs aching, and stomachs rumbling. MadRiver cooks some stew on his portable stove while I put fresh clothes on Alex. Soon after eating, Alex crawls into her sleeping bag and falls silent. She doesn't move for eleven straight hours.

The morning is bright, our socks are dry, and our attitudes are cheery. We leave the shelter in fine spirits after a peaceful night's sleep and immediately encounter an unrecognizable river.

We did, of course, cross this water yesterday. Then, however, it resembled a brook. Now it looks like a crazy rush of water flying over a multitude of submerged rocks with alarming speed. None of the stepping stones Alex previously used are visible. MadRiver and I look at each other with concern, and I am grateful I have enough food to sustain us for another day. If we can't safely cross, then we'll have to hole up for another night at the shelter.

One can't step casually through such water. It can, if you're not extremely careful, knock you off your feet and slam your head into a dozen rocks as it carries you down the mountain. My eyes scan the surface as I weigh the risks. Should we just hang out at the shelter for a few more hours and see if the water level diminishes throughout the day?

I notice MadRiver unbuckling his pack and I give him a curious look. He nods at me before taking a careful step into the water. He's going to give it a try. The unfastened buckles are a precaution. If the water knocks him off balance, he will attempt to ditch his pack before it snags on something and forces his head underwater.

MadRiver moves slowly and carefully, using his hiking poles for support and balance. There are a few places where the water rises above his thighs, but, for the most part, it's only knee deep. He reaches the other side without incident, then turns and looks at me.

I take Alex's pack from her, then tell her to sit down

and wait for me to return. My strategy: get my back-pack and Alex's backpack across, then return for Alex. This will give me a chance to experiment with my footing and look for the easiest places for Alex to step. I am not allowed to carry her, as that would disqualify her for the Four Thousand Footer Club. She has to hike every step on her own two feet. Alex will walk across *if* I think it safe for her to do so.

I unbuckle my straps, sling Alex's pack over my wrist, and step into the cold water.

The force of the moving water is surprising. Even though I'm only up to my ankles and standing immediately next to dry land, my feet are roughly shoved by the current. In go my hiking poles. I anchor them between stones and start to shuffle my feet, taking small steps to better secure my balance.

I'm halfway across when I come to a depression in the bottom of the brook. My next step submerges me up to my thighs, and I must move extremely slowly so that I don't lose my balance. The depression is only a few feet wide, but it presents a danger for Alex. Water up to my thighs means water up to Alex's chest, and this water is extremely cold and moving fast.

When I reach MadRiver, I turn and wave at Alex, who smiles and patiently waves back.

"I'm going to need your help," I say.

"Sure. What can I do?"

I ask if he'll meet me halfway with Alex and spot us as we go through the deeper part of the water. He agrees, and we carefully wade through the rushing brook until we reach the middle. He anchors his poles between rocks and grips the handles tightly as I return to Alex.

I explain to her that the water is very cold, and that she will feel as though her legs are being strongly pushed. I tell her that in order to keep her balance, she must move very slowly, and she must bring her feet through the water instead of trying to bring each foot up and over with every step. I also tell her that I will keep a firm hand on her at all times. She nods, then looks at MadRiver standing in the middle of the brook.

"He's going to help us across a deeper part of the stream. When we get close to where he is, you must listen to me and do exactly what I tell you without question."

Alex agrees.

"One more thing. Always respect the water. It can knock you down and carry you away if you become too quick or too careless. Respect the situation we're in."

"Got it," she says. I grip her upper arm, and we start to cross.

I feel wonderful without my backpack and certain of where to step since I've just crossed the brook twice. Alex is nervous at first; I can feel her arm shaking within my fingers as she takes her first few steps. Her breath comes quickly, loudly.

"You okay?"

"Yeah," she breathes as her eyes dart here and there.

"Just keep your feet in the water and take slow, small steps. I won't let you go."

"Promise?" she asks. I can feel the hairs of her arm standing up; they tickle the sides of my gripping fingers.

"Promise." My hold on her is unyielding. We inch our way toward MadRiver, who patiently waits on the other side of the gap, his hands gripping the two poles that are anchored in the rocks around him.

"What if I fall?" she asks.

"Then I fall with you," I answer. "So don't fall."

We reach the depression in a few careful minutes. The water has not yet touched the bottom of Alex's shorts, though her knees are now fully submerged.

MadRiver stands three feet away. I look at him and raise my eyebrows. He gives a small nod, then stretches out his hand, ready to assist.

"Alex, this is the part that's too deep for you." The rushing water competes with my voice and I must raise my tone in order to be heard. "Between here and where MadRiver is standing, the water goes up to your chest." Alex's eyes grow wide.

"I want you to stay here while I step down."

Alex looks worried, but says nothing.

Keeping my hold on Alex, I step down and feel the frigid water touch the bottom of my hiking shorts.

"When I tell you to, I want you to jump toward MadRiver. I will have your arm and I will not let it go until MadRiver has you."

Bracing myself, I nod to MadRiver, then tell Alex to go for it.

She immediately jumps. There is a split second between my letting go and MadRiver's catching her—but then he's got her, and she's safe in his arms. He guides her body toward a sturdy rock and places her back in the water. The two then wade hand in hand toward the other side of the crossing while my heart vacates my throat and descends to its proper place.

Wet feet, wet boots, wet knees. At least it's all downhill hiking from here. The three of us chat amicably, then Alex and I go ahead of MadRiver while he takes a break to answer the call of nature.

There's something I'm supposed to be remembering; there's something that's at the back of my mind that I can't quite bring to the forefront. No matter, I tell myself. Whatever it is, it can wait until we're happily back at the car.

And then that infernal grouse steps out directly in front of my left foot.

Ah yes. *That's* what I was supposed to remember.

I place my hiking pole between me and it, and I tell Alex to stay back. Curiously, I am not frightened. MadRiver is several tenths of a mile away, and LRiz is no longer around to sacrifice. It's just me, Alex, and this bugger of a little bird, who is actually trying to get around me to peck at my daughter! There is no room for fear, for I am alone with a kid to protect.

The grouse keeps bird-stepping toward Alex, who stays behind me while the bird and I circle each other. Finally, the three of us rotate so far that Alex and I end up standing on the side of the path closest to our car, while the bird stands between us and the trail we've just traveled. My daughter and I retreat from the bird slowly, stepping backward, not showing it our backs. The grouse's fussing grows louder as we increase the distance between us and it. When the bird is convinced of its apparent success, it turns and triumphantly shuffles back into the woods.

MadRiver shows up a little while later. I ask if he saw the grouse, and he says no. I tell him what happened, and he laughs at us. I resist the temptation to whack him with my hiking stick.

The car. The car! The beautiful car. There it stands, with all its promise of transportation to dry and cozy places. I help Alex take off her pack. She dances a short jig of relief before throwing herself prostrate on the ground.

Little Things Matter (a Lot)

Peaks #40–#42: The Bonds, July 10, 2009

Wup! Alex pokes at the shadow of her hundredth bug and watches as it promptly disappears. We're inside our tent at Guyot Campsite, more than seven miles from a road and deep within the heart of the White Mountain National Forest. We've spent the day climbing three of the New Hampshire Forty-eight's most remote mountains, 4,540-foot West Bond, 4,698-foot Mount Bond, and 4,265-foot Bondcliff, and now we're playing our favorite camping game, bop the bug.

We're not literally bopping bugs, of course. To do so would run contrary to Alex's good nature. Instead, we wait for a bug to land on the top of our tent, then we poke at it from underneath. We take great delight in watching the dark form disappear and then reappear somewhere else, at which point we promptly poke it again. There are usually multiple insects to harass at any given moment, so the game is often quick paced and frenetic. Giggles fill our tent as she and I collide elbows in our effort to outdo each other.

It's a lovely ending to a beautiful, but curious, day. The three mountains we hiked, collectively known as the Bonds, are considered the crown jewels of the Whites. Far from towns and highways, the view from the top of each offers a pure and natural vista. After reading about these hikes, I had eagerly anticipated standing on the tops of all three Bonds with Alex. I'd thought she might be impressed by landscapes unmarred by human activity. Aside from the tips of Mount Washington's summit structures and perhaps a bit of a distant resort's ski slopes, we should see nothing but trees, valleys, and rocks.

Alex had enjoyed the day, but not as much as I'd hoped. West Bond went well. The hike from Guyot Campsite to the summit is just more than half a mile, and the trail meanders through dense woods before topping out on a bare peak. The forest kept us cool under the intense morning sun, and the views from the top were spectacular. Alex was appropriately impressed, and we descended West Bond eager to see what the other two Bonds had to offer.

We made it to Mount Bond's summit about forty-five minutes after having left West Bond. The day was warm, but not overly so. Alex was humming one of her made-up tunes, and my back felt deliriously light. We'd left most of our gear at the campsite, since we'd be spending another night there after coming back from today's peaks; ascending without my overstuffed backpack was a delight. As we climbed the last few feet to Mount Bond's summit, I decided that I would visually scour the wilderness and try to locate some kind of man-made structure. Were the guidebooks correct? Can you really see nothing but nature up there, save the tips of the towers on Washington?

Once up top, I turned to my right and searched the landscape. Nope, no man-made structures in this direction. I turned to my left. No signs of human life in that direction, either. I turned a complete 180 degrees and focused on the valley below. No roads cut through the greenery, and no buildings marred the fields. I scanned the mountaintops. There were no signs of human impact: just cliffs, ravines, peaks, and sky. Hallelujah. I breathed in deeply, fully appreciating that this mountain was one of those rare, uncontaminated places, one of those very few spots in the American Northeast where one can truly get away from the trappings of human society. This was Mount Bond, the most remote peak in the Whites.

This was Mount Bond, a place Alex desperately wished to vacate.

At first, she loved the view. I heard a fair amount of oohing and aahing as we made our way up the summit cone. I saw her stand on a boulder and turn steadily around, taking everything in, appreciating the wild panorama. For a moment, she appeared to be just as enamored as I was. Then, unfortunately, she looked down, and all her happiness evaporated.

A dying bumblebee was struggling to crawl across the boulder. A very large, very bristly bumblebee. Alex stared at it, having forgotten all about the scenery. Fascinated by the sad plight of the insect, she watched as it tried to fight off the inevitable. The bee looked as though it were seconds away from meeting its Maker. Thankfully, its form was full and intact; it had not been stepped on, so at least Alex's sorrow would not be contaminated with guilt.

The top of Mount Bond is spacious, and there were plenty of other rocks on which to relax, so I suggested we choose another area for our lunch break. Alex reluctantly complied and finally tore her eyes from the insect, which had stopped moving and was probably well on its way toward the light at the end of the tunnel.

Alex was downcast for a few minutes, but she seemed to perk up a bit after I filled her hands with a large peanut butter sandwich. By the time she had swallowed her last sticky mouthful, her usual smile had returned, and her eyes once again scanned the horizon. When we rose to tackle Bondcliff, our third and final mountain of the day, her spirits appeared fully restored.

The path between Mount Bond and Bondcliff is above tree line. A hiker has unobstructed views, and therefore Bondcliff's jagged and rocky flank is visible at all times. To me, that flank was breathtaking, and I couldn't believe I had the good fortune to be up there with my daughter. Alex, usually eager to gaze upon nature's wonders, had a completely different kind of emotional experience.

"Spiders!" she exclaimed, staring at her feet.

We had stopped for a water break. Though getting to Bondcliff from Mount Bond requires just over a mile of hiking, the day was bright with summer sunshine, and there was no shade to be found. Alex stood with her fingers gripped tightly around the cap of her Nalgene, looking balefully down at the dirt between her boots.

A line of spiders scuttled across the path beneath us, single file. As red as measles and as small as drops of rain, the critters trickled down the trail as though following one another to an annual arachnid ball. Though Alex isn't afraid of one spider all by itself, the sight of so many at once unsettled her, and she refused to look up again until we had carefully stepped over and around the multitude. Once past, we steadfastly made our way up the rocky trail until we stood on the tallest rock.

The views from the top of Bondcliff were every bit as good as the views from Mount Bond. Both mountains, as well as West Bond, had been, in my opinion, spectacular. As we retraced our steps over Mount Bond, then past the trail to West Bond, and then finally down to our campsite, Alex and I chatted about how great the weather was, how spectacular the views had been, and how much we both looked forward to heating up a can of soup. As we kicked off our boots and put on our camp sandals, I asked Alex if these were now her favorite mountains. To my great surprise, she immediately responded in the negative.

"No! I didn't really like them all that much."

"Really? Why not?"

"The bumblebee."

All that good stuff, overshadowed by one dying bumblebee?

"But Alex, what about the views?"

"Oh yeah, the views were nice. Especially on West Bond. I did like West Bond. West Bond didn't have a hurt bumblebee."

"But you didn't care for the other two?"

"No, not really."

"Because of the bumblebee."

"Yeah."

"But there wasn't a bumblebee on Bondcliff."

"Yeah, but there were spiders."

"Alex, you've seen spiders on trails before. You've never cared about them on other hikes."

"But there were so many of them this time! Where were they all going? Why were they all in a line? That freaked me out."

"The very top of Bondcliff didn't have any spiders on it," I pointed out.

"Yes, but I was worried the whole time we were up there. I thought I'd see more spiders."

The Bonds, cream of the White Mountain crop, tainted by a bunch of spiders and one dying bumblebee. An adult wouldn't have given these creatures a second thought. An adult would have become too overwhelmed with the scenery to notice the bugs below. I smiled at Alex and admired her ability to focus on the so-called little things. Even if such focus does cause her grief at times, an appreciation of details is a gift. The more one can notice and see, the more one can intensely experience life.

Now, half an hour later and safely sequestered inside our two-person tent, Alex has nothing to fret over. She can see neither bee nor spider nor mosquito. *Wup!* There goes another one. Alex laughs with delight, and then floors me by declaring this the "best day ever."

Wait a minute. Now I'm confused.

I don't want to spoil her positive mood, but I'm too curious not to ask. "What about the bumblebee and the spiders?"

"Oh . . . well, this makes up for it," she says before poking at the shadow of yet another unfortunate bug.

Such is the mind of a six-year-old, I guess.

I smile and join Alex at her bug bopping.

We Can't Always Make It Better

Peak #44: Owl's Head, July 25–26, 2009

A lex, climb over! Now!"

My patience is rapidly vanishing, for the mosquitoes are unbearable. We're being dive-bombed by the nasty critters, and I simply cannot stand still for one second longer. She needs to get over that log, pronto.

"I can't!" Alex wails.

MadRiver throws me an uncharacteristic look of impatience.

"Alex, just do it! We're being eaten alive here!"

"But they're everywhere!" Alex protests, referring not to the bugs, but to the giant bundles of moving mucus covering the bark in front of her. The slugs are massive, the biggest I've ever seen. At least five inches long and three pencils thick, they are swollen, slimy, and the color of rotten orange peels. MadRiver and I noticed them when we stepped over this fallen tree five minutes ago, but we were too consumed with the menacing mosquitoes to fully appreciate their unpleas-antness. Alex, however, reached the log and came to a dead stop. At six years old, she is much shorter than we are and therefore closer to the ground. The top of the log MadRiver and I casually stepped over is level with her waist. She now stands staring helplessly at the not-so-little creatures, refusing to move.

It's late July, and Alex and I are closing in on our goal. This mountain, 4,025-foot Owl's Head, is num-ber forty-four out of forty-eight. It's one of the more challenging peaks, as the summit is located nine miles away from civilization and the trail leading to it goes through a few potentially dangerous water crossings. I have once again enlisted the aid of MadRiver, as I do not want to venture so far into the wilderness with-out the company of at least one other adult. In addi-tion to trusty MadRiver, a fellow with the trail name of Dave Bear, an affable New Hampshire native and all-around outdoorsman, will meet us about a mile from the summit. The four of us plan to reach the top of the mountain, then descend the summit cone and camp.

This morning, MadRiver and I decided to go off the trail and navigate a straight line through the woods in order to spare Alex the water crossings. We should eventually pop back out on the trail close to the summit cone. Unfortunately, going off-trail turned out to be a more serious endeavor than I had anticipated. The veg-etation is thick and full of spiderwebs, and pushing our way through the never-ending series of branches has done quite a number on our energy and good spirits. Mosquitoes have been our constant companions, successfully avoiding our swats and landing on our skin at every opportunity. Mud has sucked at our boots and pulled them off on more than one occasion. It's been a difficult time in the woods, and I will be extremely happy to reach the end of this so-called shortcut and step back onto a maintained trail. I've already decided, without asking Alex, that we will take our chances with the water crossings on our way out tomorrow. I've fed enough mosquitoes on this hike, and my daughter has evidently seen enough slugs.

I step back to the log and survey the bark. There, to her right, is a bare spot, free of slug and slime. "Alex, look, step there."

"What if I stumble and squish one?"

"Then it'll just have to squish," I say, my tone rising as I feel yet another mosquito bite the back of my neck. The incessant *buzzing* is getting to me; she has to get over this friggin' log already so we can get out of here.

"But I don't want to kill any of them!" she cries.

Ah . . . so that's it. Part of my frustration was my confusion at Alex's refusal to move. Never before had she behaved as though she were repulsed by a living creature. She's a friend to all, be it bird, butterfly, or bumblebee. Evidently she's a friend to slugs too. Her hesitation is not due to fear; it's due to concern.

"Just hold on to my hand as you step. I'll make sure you don't slip, fall, or stumble."

I stretch my hand out to her. Alex does not take it.

"Honey, do you want to climb this peak or not?" More buzzing, more biting. My question is gentle, but I feel I'm close to losing my cool. Call me cruel, but I would happily sacrifice all the slugs on the planet just to get away from this particular bit of forest.

Her hand grips mine, and I pull her up and over. She doesn't stumble; she doesn't fall. The slugs carry on in peace, their slimy, swollen shapes unsullied.

I look over at MadRiver, who is staring at Alex with a look of surprise. He's just witnessed a rare occurrence of Alex acting her very young age, and the scene has shocked him speechless. He gets over his astonishment enough to give my daughter an encouraging smile as she approaches, then he turns and continues to trudge in a north-northwest direction.

The longest hour of my life later, we emerge from the forest and step onto a nice, clear path. Alex lets out a whoop of relief. Our way no longer impeded by branches, mud, or slugs, we hurry up the trail, relieved to be finished with that portion of the ascent.

Dave Bear stands waiting a few hundred yards up, and together the four of us search for a place to set up our tents. Eventually we discover a spot wide enough to accommodate us, and we spend the next hour preparing the evening's sleeping quarters. Once camp is made, we head for the Owl's Head slide.

The first few tenths of a mile go well enough. It's a bit of a challenge, but we expected as much. We are, after all, walking up the site of an old landslide. The grade is steep, the footing is difficult, and bits of scree—loose rock mixed with dirt—go tumbling down the slope with our every step. Alertness and great caution are key. One misstep might send us sliding down the mountain on a carpet of moving pebbles.

Alex is in front, climbing slowly and carefully, finding her way up the slope. The path up the summit cone is neither blazed nor adorned with cairns, as the peak lies in a protected wilderness area where no official trails are permitted to exist. In spite of the lack of markers, the path is fairly easy to discern. There's only one direction to go when climbing a slide: up.

We're doing well. The day is warm, but not unbearably so. Alex appears strong in spite of having already hiked eight miles. It seems we're going to make it to the top and back down to our tents with plenty of time to spare before nightfall. Owl's Head isn't really so tough, especially when one takes two days to hike it instead of one. The bushwhack wasn't much fun, true, but overall, things are going much better than I had anticipated.

Until now.

We are two-tenths of a mile above the base of the slide when Alex freezes above me and lets out a small gasp. I look up to discover the cause of her abrupt lack of motion, then I freeze and let out my own gasp.

There's a young moose standing to the left of us, just

a dozen or so yards above our heads. Its front hooves are planted in the exposed and loose scree of the slide while its hind legs remain in the shelter of the trees beyond. It's just standing there, unmoving, looking like a curious contribution from a peakbagging taxidermist.

"Look at the moose!" a man and a woman call from about fifty feet above us. They are distracted by this unexpected sight and are descending rapidly and carelessly in their excitement. Scree pours down the trail as their feet kick into the slide, and I avert my eyes to prevent dust and gravel from injuring them. The couple's footsteps come to a halt, and the stream of scree slows to a trickle. Looking up, I see them level with the moose, on the other side of the slide. I suppress a groan as I realize what they're about to do. Sure enough, the man and woman start to edge toward the moose, big grins on their faces.

"Stay where you are," I murmur to Alex, though there's no need for me to do so. My daughter knows better; she would never purposely walk toward a wild animal. I watch the couple advance in the direction of the juvenile with dread, fervently hoping their folly does not result in someone getting hurt or killed.

As a general rule, moose don't attack people in the Whites. They prefer to avoid the company of humans and will usually leave an area as soon as they hear someone approaching. That being said, moose are large, unpredictable animals. In other parts of the country, people have been trampled to death after making the mistake of getting too close for the moose's comfort. Though this particular specimen is a juvenile, it's still large enough to inflict some serious damage should it decide to knock someone over. Also, and more important, where is its mother? If Mama Moose is nearby, then we all might be in for a very interesting afternoon.

Alex and I remain motionless, feet stuck to the side of the rock slide as the couple come to a stop immediately next to the young creature. The man reaches out his hand to touch its back (*What are you doing!* I inwardly scream)—and nothing happens. The moose doesn't move. It doesn't even flinch. It just stands there, looking straight out at the valley, as though it had decided to amble on up and take in the view. No Mama Moose comes crashing out of the trees to drive away the strangers; no one comes stomping to its rescue.

Something's obviously wrong. Why is this young animal just standing there?

Wanting to put some distance between Alex and this scenario, I whisper, "Let's go." We climb past the couple as quickly and as quietly as we can, sticking to the opposite side of the slide. Dave Bear and MadRiver follow. After a few minutes, we stop to look down. The other hikers have resumed their descent, leaving the moose standing in its fixed position.

"What's going on with that moose?" Alex asks. "I don't know," I answer. MadRiver and Dave Bear both shrug when I turn to them. We continue our climb.

Two hours later, the moose is still there. We're on

our way down from the wooded and viewless summit, feeling tired but satisfied at having checked off another peak, when the brown, four-legged figure appears beneath us, in exactly the same location it occupied during our ascent. The poor youngster continues to stare blankly out into the distance as we descend toward it. Alex becomes unnerved.

"What's wrong with it? Where's its mama?" she asks, her voice trembling. "Did she die?"

The two of us sit down on a small ledge and watch as Dave Bear and MadRiver slowly pass the creature without incident. The moose appears catatonic, unable to recognize or care about our existence.

"Poor moose," Alex says in a small voice. "Why isn't it moving? Why is it alone? Can we give it some water? It must be hot, standing there in the sun."

I gently explain that there is nothing we can do. We *could* try to get it to drink some water out of our bottles, but then what would happen to the moose tomorrow? And the day after tomorrow? And the day after that? We are more than eight miles from any road. We can't physically carry the moose down the slide, and any attempt to move it might make its physical situation even worse. In the end, all we can do is inform the forest rangers. If there is anything to be done, then they will do it.

"Will they get a veterinarian to hike up here and fix it?"

Alex looks so very sad. I want to tell her yes, that there will be someone arriving to rescue the moose, that we humans have the power to take away all the cruel aspects of nature. I want to tell her that life is always beautiful and that nothing ever happens without good reason.

Instead, I tell her the truth.

"No, honey. I doubt they'll send anyone. Nature must take its course."

"What does that mean?" she asks as she wipes an eye.

"It means that we can't fix all the hurt animals in nature. That nature has a way of balancing itself out. That trying to calm an injured moose in order to fix it is probably extremely difficult and perhaps impossible."

"But where is its mama?"

I hate this. Nature is cruel. Young moose are

sometimes separated from their mothers, for all kinds of reasons, and then they sometimes wither away and die. Life is full of pain. I don't want my daughters to ever really know this or understand it, but they must. It is the way things are. To sugarcoat reality is to lie, and I don't lie to my children.

I look down and see MadRiver and Dave Bear patiently waiting below. I carefully stand and start to move toward them. Alex follows close behind me, glumly eyeing the moose as we pass it.

"I don't know what happened to its mama, Alex. Maybe she became injured or was killed. Maybe she left, thinking it was time for her baby to go off on its own. I don't know."

We pass the moose easily, reach our companions, and descend the rest of the slide in silence.

Alex is quiet throughout much of dinner, saying only a few polite words to MadRiver and Dave Bear. Later, after we've hung our food bags high in the trees (to keep them from bears) and snuggled into our sleeping bags, Alex breaks her silence.

"Would you ever leave me?" she asks.

"No," I assure her.

"What if I was sick?"

"Then I would take care of you."

"What if I was mean to you all the time?"

"Well, I wouldn't appreciate your attitude, but I'd stay anyway."

"What if I got lost?"

"I would come and find you."

"What if you couldn't?"

"I would."

"But Mama, what if you *couldn't*?"

"I would never stop trying, Alex. I would keep looking until I found you, even if it took years."

Alex mulls this over for a moment. Then she asks, "Why do you think that moose wasn't with its mother?"

"I don't know. Maybe the mama thought it was time for the young one to live on its own. Or perhaps she became sick."

Night has fallen, and Alex's face is difficult to make out. She's quiet, and for a few minutes I think she has fallen asleep. My mind starts to drift, and I'm a second away from slumber before her voice drives away the sandman.

"How many slugs do you think we've killed?"

"What?" The oddity of the question fully wakes me, and I sit up in my sleeping bag.

"Slugs. On the trail. We've probably stepped on some and not noticed."

Sighing, I agree with her. "We probably have, sure. Though I don't know how many."

More silence. I lie back down, wondering when the next question will come. I don't have to wait long.

"You promise you won't ever leave me, Mama?"

I reach for Alex's sleeping bag and pull it toward

me. Wrapping my arms around my daughter, I assure her that I'll never make her leave our house before she is an adult. I tell her that I'll always take care of her when she's sick. I tell her that for the rest of my life, I will be there for her whenever she needs me. Alex lies still while I voice my reassurances. She seems content when I finish my statements, for her snores fill our tent shortly thereafter.

Enjoy the Journey While It Lasts

Peak #48: Mount Moosilauke, August 30, 2009

When I left my PhD program at Harvard University to become a stay-at-home mom, the vast majority of people in my life thought I was insane. More than a few women declared me the Antifeminist, and most of my friends avoided me like the plague. Leave Harvard? For motherhood? Didn't I know that people would give their right arm to attend Harvard, the most prestigious academic institution in the world? Couldn't I just be a proper modern-day woman, stick my babies in day care, and stay the course?

Inevitably, the question would come up in conversation: "You're going to go back and finish when the kids get a little older, right?" At first, my answer was "Maybe." Then, after a few years, my answer was "No, we're going to homeschool." I wanted to give my children the opportunity of a truly individualized education, I didn't want to lose them to peer pressure and group-think and low academic standards.

Now, not only was I the Antifeminist, but a very strange antifeminist whose children would undoubtedly grow up without the benefit of "socialization" (learning how to navigate peer pressure and avoid bullies). When it became clear that no, I was not returning to Harvard, and no, I was not going to put my daughters in a public or private school, every single person I had known before I became pregnant promptly dropped out of my life. They could no longer relate to who I was, or to what I felt I needed to do.

Six years later, I am driving toward Mount Moosilauke on the morning of our final 4K hike, looking back at my decision and congratulating myself for making the right choice for me. I am not one to prescribe my own values onto other parents, so my feelings have nothing to do with self-righteousness. My joy stems from the knowledge that had I stayed at Harvard and put the kids in day care, then later in preschool, I would never have come to know them as well as I do now. I would have ended up too busy, too stressed for time, too cranky.

The years go by so fast. Just last week, Alex was taking her first steps. Just yesterday, Sage was an infant. Today, both girls are going up Mount Moosilauke, a 4,802-foot mountain. Sage will probably walk halfway before asking to be carried (I'll gladly oblige). Alex, of course, will hike unassisted.

We'll have a crowd with us this morning, August 30, 2009, the day that Alex becomes one of the youngest ever to summit, on foot, all forty-eight of New Hampshire's highest mountains. To my great surprise, many hikers are either ascending with us or meeting us at the top. I had been aware that Alex was becoming well known throughout the New Hampshire hiking community via my blog, but I'd had no idea that so many folks would actually come out to show their support. I am grateful to them all, for I know Alex will take great delight in meeting so many other hikers and hearing their congratulations. The mother in me wants the whole world to come and applaud my worthy daughter. The hiker in me recognizes that these folks are kind to take a day off their usual weekend schedules to ascend Mount Moosilauke with a kid they barely know. They are displaying a giant act of kindness. My emotions begin to get the best of me, and I blink away a few sappy tears.

"Hey, I recognize this!" Alex exclaims from the backseat of our Honda Civic.

"What?" Sage asks beside her.

"This road! There were moose standing on it last time!"

"Really? That must have been exciting," Hugh responds, twisting around from the passenger seat to smile at her.

We're carefully winding our way along curvy and rural Route 118, the same road we used to first approach Mount Moosilauke eight months ago, on a cold mid-December day. We had come upon two moose standing in the middle of the road that morning, licking salt from the pavement in the wake of a snowplow. I had to wait for the moose to move of their own accord, which meant Alex and I sat and admired them for a good five minutes. That was the day we came within a few hundred yards of the summit before having to turn back. That was the day we first fully understood the importance of windproof gloves, the day that Alex learned it's better to retreat than to risk injury. The day we were both introduced to the glory of "butt sliding" down a snowy trail. We certainly had a grand time last winter, not only getting used to but also enjoying the layering and delayering process, the use of microspikes and snowshoes, the feel of balaclavas and face masks. Alex claims those were her favorite hiking months. I wonder . . . will she still want to get out there this coming winter, after her quest is over? Does she love hiking enough to continue after this mission is complete? Will she be just as much of a hiker tomorrow as she is today?

I turn onto Ravine Lodge Road, the narrow street that leads to Moosilauke Ravine Lodge and the Gorge Brook Trail. This trail had not been an option last December, since Ravine Road is gated during the winter; we had driven all the way to the other side of the mountain and used the Glencliff Trail to ascend. Today, we are able to access the more popular and easier route to the summit.

I reach the lodge, find a parking space, and turn off the engine. Both girls burst into a fit of excited and uncontrollable giggles. Alex chortles with gleeful pride while Sage chuckles with genuine affection for her sister. They are pumped and ready to roll.

Hugh does not share his daughters' merriment, as he is too apprehensive about his own ascent. This will be his first 4K, and he is unsure of the time it will take him to reach the top. To ensure he does not slow the group down, he will get an early start and, if we don't catch up with him somewhere along the trail, meet us just beneath the summit. I assure him that he is welcome to hike with everyone else, and that we will stop and wait for him if the need arises, but he gives an additional reason for insisting upon an early departure. For maximum comfort, he wears capri-style pants, which expose his artificial limbs. Though Hugh never minds people knowing he's an amputee and, in fact, is happy to answer questions about his prostheses, he does not want to take today's focus away from Alex. After tightening a few nuts and bolts, he wishes Alex good luck and sets off on his own.

Hugh. We couldn't have done this without his help. He has shown an enormous amount of trust and faith in me. Not every man would support his wife in taking their very young daughter into the wilderness alone.

He has happily taken care of Sage while Alex and I traipsed through the mountains, and he's been a huge advocate of our quest.

MadRiver and his beautiful wife, Susan, arrive at the parking lot while I am rummaging through my trunk for Alex's backpack. Susan is a few years younger than her husband and is very fit, with long blonde hair and a beautiful face. She's every bit as sweet as she is gorgeous. Both my girls have taken a strong liking to her, just as they have taken a liking to her husband, MadRiver. The two of them have become my daughters' New Hampshire aunt and uncle, in spite of MadRiver's continual insistence that he doesn't really like children.

On the heels of MadRiver comes Karen, an affable lady who has hiked with us twice before. She and MadRiver will assist with my gear. They will carry most of the contents of my backpack so that I can put Sage in there when she becomes unable or unwilling to hike any farther on her own two feet.

Sage. My beautiful youngest child. She has been so patient and understanding of Mama's time away. If there is anything I regret about the past year and a half, it's been the time away from my littlest girl. That has been the price of this adventure, for I now feel somewhat distanced from her, as though I have lost an important amount of time that can never be made up.

More people are arriving now. There's a group of ten around us, most of whom I know only from the Internet. I put trail names to faces as they introduce themselves, and Alex greets each and every one with a huge smile on her face. Her day has come, and she is thrilled.

I kneel and draw Sage into my arms. "Would you like to go camping with me next weekend? Just you and me, on our own?" I ask.

Her cute little face splits into a grin. "Yeah," she answers in her squeaky, high-pitched voice. I resolve, right then and there, to spend the next year taking Sage hiking or camping almost every weekend, just as I've done with Alex. We don't have to do 4Ks. We don't even have to do mountains. There are water-falls to visit, ponds to explore, hills to climb. We just need to get out there, she and I, the two of us. I've missed her.

The time has come. The mountain beckons. More than a dozen people accompany us as we set our boots on the trail. Other hikers will arrive at the trailhead an hour or so later and catch up with us; still others will ascend different routes and greet us at the summit. There are so many well-wishers, so many friendly folks to chat up Alex, myself, one another. Our group moves along the trail at a relaxed pace, Sage skipping ahead with MadRiver, the two of them walking ahead of the crowd. Alex hikes in the center of the hubbub and converses with a sister-brother duo, the daughter and son of a fellow hiker. These children are nine and six years old, and this will be their third 4K. I hear snippets of their happy back-and-forth, getting-to-know-you questions. "Where do you live?" "How old are you?" "Do you have any other brothers or sisters?" "What's your favorite mountain?"

It's a perfect day. The temperature is just right, and the bugs are behaving themselves. We quickly reach the halfway point: a tree bearing a sign marked Last Water, standing tall over the bubbling Gorge Brook. We take a break here, though there is barely enough room in the small clearing to hold everyone in our group. Water bottles are refilled, snacks are consumed, and the crowd continues its happy chatter. When we ready ourselves to leave, Sage tells me she is tired and asks to be carried. I place my empty backpack on the ground and hold it steady while she climbs in.

Apart from coming to me for the occasional snack, Alex has thus far remained with her newfound friends. This is to be expected, as she is a bright, friendly, and lively child. I had never thought she'd stay by my side during this, our final 4K hike. Not with so many agreeable faces surrounding her, not with so many opportunities for cheerful chatter.

Though I am happy for her, I feel a twinge of sadness. So many hikes together, just her and me. So many memories. The time Alex discovered she had a live inchworm on her tongue and spat it onto a nearby leaf, where it inched away, unharmed. The time I walked face-first into a large, bug-filled spiderweb, and Alex shrieked with both laughter and alarm. The time we saw bear tracks in the mud in front of us and spent the following hour walking with hammering hearts, hoping never to see the actual bear (we didn't). The many times we sang Monty Python songs to make steep sections a little easier, the many times we made up stories to get us through the final mile back to the car, the many times we counted slugs on giant slabs of granite.

Today's hike is nothing like the ones that have come before. There are so many people with us! I am grateful to them all for being here, for this is how it should be. My daughter deserves this grand celebration. However, in my mind, our shared 4K quest has already come to an end, for our mother-daughter duo days are in the past.

The hike just previous to this one, the last mountain Alex and I ascended on our own, had been a quiet and pleasant climb up Mount Flume on Franconia Ridge. We walked the lovely and well-maintained Osseo Trail in peaceful harmony. Alex enjoyed that hike, especially the upper part of the trail with its many wooden ladders. When we arrived on the bare and rocky summit, I lifted her into the air and let out a *whoo-hoo!* of victory. I knew, standing there, that that would be my last moment alone with my wonderful five-turned-six-year-old peakbagging daughter, and I wanted to relish every second of it. After putting Alex down, I opened my pack and removed two chocolate whoopie pies, a departure from our usual candy bars. The two of us then sat side by side and ate, feeling wonderful and carefree in the warm summer sun.

"Alex," I had said after swallowing a mouthful of the deliciously sweet confection, "thanks for doing this with me."

Alex looked at me, chocolate crumbs on her lips and cheeks, her face quizzical.

"Why are you thanking me?" she asked.

"Because you've put up with me. With all of my nagging and hovering and *be careful*s."

Alex gave me a huge smile. "You're welcome. I really love being out here. I wish we could live high up in the mountains."

Then we said nothing more, but simply sat and chewed our whoopie pies in the gloriously fresh mountain air.

We're on the move again, and oh my, is Sage heavy! Her weight is not evenly distributed, as she crouches low in the backpack in an effort to make herself comfortable. I make it half a mile before my spine begins to give way. A member of our group, a kind man named Tim, offers to carry her for me, and I gratefully acquiesce. A couple tenths of a mile later, Sage's snores tell us that her efforts to make herself comfortable have succeeded. Her lolling head protrudes out the top of

the untied main compartment, and her blonde, wispy hair flies every which way as Tim steps over rocks, roots, and mud.

We're almost above tree line now, just a little while longer and we'll have the summit in our sights. One of Alex's new friends, the six-year-old boy, complains of being tired. His father encourages him onward. *We're almost there . . . you can do it . . . I'm so proud of you.* It's a gentle push, with an offer to sit and rest for a few moments before ascending the remainder of the trail. The two lag behind while the boy drags his feet, but his pace quickens after a few minutes, and he soon catches up with Alex.

I love witnessing gentle pushes, for I think that children are far more capable than most adults realize. Sometimes they just need to be reminded of their own strength. When some parents take it too far, turning the push into a shove, that's another matter. Those are the ones with small children sitting in the middle of the trail, begging to turn around and crying because their legs are too tired to go any farther. I've never actually seen that occur in the Whites. While gentle pushes are good, it's important to respect kids' feelings as to when and what they want to hike. This boy today: he's tired, no doubt, and he may think he just can't do it anymore. But the truth is, he can, and his father knows he can. More important, the boy *wants* to reach the summit. So, far from expecting too much of him, the father is helping his son realize his potential.

Sage wakes as soon as we step above tree line. We stop so Tim can take her out of the backpack, as she's more than capable of walking these last few tenths of a mile.

This is it. I can see the peak a quarter of a mile away, a large jumble of massive boulders under a blue and cloudless sky. Dark silhouettes move about up there, early arrivals waiting for Alex to ascend. A few dozen yards ahead of us, a familiar figure leans against a tall cairn. It is Hugh, who arrived at this point an hour ago and is waiting to summit with the rest of us. Alex runs to him and leaps into his arms. Sage follows and throws herself around his knees.

Time for the final push. Alex leads the way, head held high, blonde hair blowing behind her in the cool mountain breeze. The crowd up top spots her and begins to cheer. Alex's pace quickens, and soon we are just below the final boulders. There are so many people! As we approach, a few kind folks line up on either side of the path and stretch their hiking poles up and over us, creating an arch under which we merrily walk. Now just fifteen feet from the summit sign, I can more clearly see the crowd that awaits us. Most of the people stand close to the high point, waiting with cameras in their hands, smiling at Alex and cheering her on. Ten feet away, then five, then two . . . Alex pulls herself up and over the final rock, stands, and touches the summit sign. The crowd bursts into noisy applause.

She's done it. My little girl's done it. All those months, all those miles, all that joyous work and happy sweat. She smiles and laughs and revels in her accomplishment, surrounded by the wonderful men and women who have hiked this mountain to show their support and make my little girl's day.

Someone tells me to get up there with her, so I do.

Cameras *click-click-click* away, people are clapping and hooting and hollering, and I am overwhelmed by—and very grateful for—all the positive attention.

B., a stout hiking enthusiast who has hiked all forty-eight of the Four Thousand Footers numerous times, approaches and hands each of us an Appalachian Mountain Club Four Thousand Footer T-shirt and me an official 4K patch. MadRiver does the honor of handing Alex her patch; she beams at him in response. As I pull Alex's shirt over her head, I ask her how she feels. "Great!" she answers. "This is better than Christmas!"

Formalities taken care of, we step down and mingle with all the lovely individuals. Alex joyfully goes from person to person, shaking hands and chatting up everyone she greets. Sage is more reserved and stays with her father, on a sunny bit of rock apart from the hubbub. At one point I go to her, hoping she is not put out by all the attention being lavished on her sister.

"How are you doing, Sage?" I ask.

"Fine."

I look at Hugh, who nods his head at all the people and smiles at me as if to say, "Go on, enjoy the moment." After kissing Sage's cheek, I leave the two of them and go back into the crowd.

The next hour is a blur of handshakes, smiles, and greetings. A few hikers give Alex presents: a compass, a stuffed animal, a bandanna. She happily accepts these items and thanks each person for their generosity. Sage also receives a gift: a stuffed animal to accompany Alex's. The girls play together, then join the other two children in a game of follow the leader, hopping from boulder to boulder and tramping along the trails.

This is the definition of Good Times. Everyone is chatting amicably, getting along, loving the mountains, and enjoying life. All is right with the world.

The second hour of celebration draws to a close, and it's time to begin the descent. Groups of people head off in every direction, taking routes of their own liking. After bidding everyone adieu, our family heads back down Gorge Brook Trail.

We leave in a group containing the two other children, their parents, MadRiver, Susan, and a few others. Sage once again rides in the backpack, now shouldered by another gracious adult whose back is much stronger than mine. Alex walks ahead of me, talking to the other kids. I'm a little 'stung.

Hey, wait! Doesn't she realize who made all this possible? Doesn't she remember who accompanied her up the other peaks? Doesn't she remember who carried all the gear and who drove to all the trailheads? Did she forget who brought all the food?

I'm not really upset, of course—the moment is just a little bittersweet. Okay, more than a little. My hiking buddy hasn't been by my side once on this hike, except for a few short minutes at the very top. She doesn't need me so much anymore. She no longer depends on me for every little thing. She's taking big steps up there, with the other kids. Steps away from me.

Our group is flying, and Sage is snoring in the backpack again, her blonde hair sticking out the top of the main compartment. Everyone is chipper as we approach the trailhead.

Wait, I'm not ready for this to be over! I want to dig in my heels and bring everyone to a screeching halt. For though I strongly suspect that Alex will continue to hike during the months and years to come, these next few minutes mark the end of something special and something uniquely ours. There won't be any more first ascents for this particular list. There won't be any more counting down or figuring out how many more weeks it will take us to finish. There also won't be any more buckling her straps, as she now knows how to fasten them herself, or tying up her bootlaces, or stretching out her microspikes, or zipping up her coat. She has become self-sufficient in all these matters and no longer requires the help of her mother. There won't be any more explanations of north, south, east or west, or of what cairns are, or of how to read a map. She understands now; she knows.

The trailhead's in sight—it's right over there! Alex has almost reached it with her new friends. I call her back. She dutifully comes to me.

"Alex, this is it—we're almost there!"

She nods her head.

"Do you mind if we reach it together? Walking side by side? It would mean a lot to me."

Alex happily grants my request, but I strongly suspect that she would prefer to end the hike with her buddies up front. This is selfish of me, I admit. I should let her go forward. I should be okay with allowing her to finish before me and without me. But I can't. There's a nasty pang in my heart that I don't like. My baby is getting older and more independent, and though I know it's my job to let her go bit by bit as the years go by, I cling to these last few moments with the despairing air of a mother who wishes the clock could tick backward.

Less than a minute later, we reach the trailhead and officially finish our quest for the New Hampshire Four Thousand Footers. I pick up Alex and kiss her on the forehead. She smiles, then asks if she can go catch up with her new friends, who are halfway across the parking lot. I give my consent, put her down, and watch as she moves away from me, strong feet crunching up the gravel as she walks into her future.

Keep Moving Forward

July 2011

Alex is now eight years old.

It's been more than three years since she and I first stood atop Mount Tecumseh, her first 4K. She wasn't yet five and a half at the time, but it never occurred to me that she couldn't ascend that mountain. I never saw her as the young girl most probably did. I saw her as she acted, as she moved, as she was capable. She was my firstborn, so everything she did seemed normal. I was proud of her, sure, but her age was just a happenstance.

Sage is now six years old, and I am extending her the same courtesy I extended Alex; I do not restrict Sage's opportunities to what popular culture deems appropriate; instead, she is free to live up to her own unique capabilities and talents. Two winters ago, when she was four, Sage decided she wanted to give Tecumseh another try. She, Alex, and I chose a sunny, relatively warm February day and played our way up the mountain. It took us six hours to ascend two miles, but we had a blast. After reaching the summit and sharing some chocolate, we sledded down packed trails amid shrieks of laughter and continual giggles. Since then, I've taken Sage hiking whenever she's asked to go. As of today, July 10, 2011, she's halfway through the Four Thousand Footer list. She also has dozens of smaller, but just as scenic, New Hampshire mountains under her belt. I am fortunate to be able to hike with her, just as I was, and still am, fortunate to be able to hike with Alex. What's important to me is not the size of the mountain scaled or the number of miles hiked, but the enjoyment of my children's company while they nurture their love of peaks.

Hiking has become our family sport, one that is shared and loved by each of us. There is, however, one serious drawback. It's something that never fails to catch me by surprise, though I probably should have gotten used to it by now. After all these months and years of hiking with one or both of my daughters, I am still taken aback by certain questions asked by the unbelieving and sometimes outraged adult. I am especially sensitive to abrasive interrogations concerning the girls' 4K accomplishments: "Do they *like* hiking?" "Do they really get up those mountains without being carried?" "Are you pushing them?" "Isn't this really all about you?"

Such questions are always voiced by strangers, by

those who have heard of the girls' hiking prowess but have never seen them on a trail. Those who have spent any amount of time hiking with us already know first-hand that Alex and Sage love to be out there, and that I don't force my kids up trails. They also know that, since the age of four, neither Alex nor Sage would allow her-self to be carried up a 4K peak. They would be highly insulted if I were to even suggest such a thing.

As for all this being about me—well, to be honest, yes and no. No, because my girls enjoy hiking, and their goals are their own. I did suggest the 4K quest to Alex, but the suggestion was made on a whim. I ini-tially thought we'd do four or five peaks a year and fin-ish when she reached the age of thirteen or fourteen; it was not immediately apparent just how strong and capable my little daughter was. Shortly after we began our quest, I realized we would be hitting the trails not once, but two to four times a month. My preparation and strong back made that possible, but the drive it-self to get out there every week, or every other week, came from Alex. Now, in the summer of 2011, the drive comes from Sage, who wants to finish the list by the end of this year. I don't see any reason to slow her down; as long as she remains happy and healthy out there, I'll support whatever she wants to do.

I would be lying, however, if I didn't admit to feel-ing immense pleasure in being there with each of my girls as they meet and exceed their own expectations. Did I love every second of Alex's 4K quest? Absolutely.

Do I treasure the times I spend with Sage as we climb over boulders and rocks? Of course! So yes, all this is for me, in the sense that I get to be with each of my daughters in outrageously beautiful settings and share moments that are intense, vibrant, and fully lived.

How to explain all this to the skeptical inquirer? How can I make the outraged individuals, those who swear that taking a kid up a mountain is akin to child abuse, understand? Is it really so difficult to believe that kids—girls in particular, for I suspect I would not be the recipient of so many questions if my children were boys—might actually enjoy hiking, and that they might possess strong abilities to pursue their passion with great interest and fortitude? Are Alex's, and now Sage's, accomplishments really that surprising?

We live in a world where it's perfectly acceptable to plop your kids down in front of a television and allow them to watch almost anything they please, for hours at a time. Video and computer games consume American culture, and the school systems keep children indoors for most of the day. Most kids are not outside for long periods of time. I must forcibly remind myself of these facts whenever I meet someone who finds Alex's story jarring.

What would happen, I wonder, if everyone threw out the television and all other forms of electronic entertainment? What would happen if parents told their kids to get outside . . . and stay there? What would happen if more moms and dads took their very young children hiking and gave them the opportunity to go as far as they liked, and at their own pace? Perhaps kids like mine really aren't so rare after all.

Alex and Sage lie on the floor of our motel room and pore over their favorite comic books. Both girls are tired from today's fifteen-mile hike up and down 5,344-foot Mount Marcy, the highest mountain in the state of New York, but they are not yet ready for bed. A huge sense of accomplishment keeps sleep at bay, for both girls have just successfully checked off their thirty-sixth state highpoint. Last summer, they stood atop the highest points of almost every state east of the American Rockies. A couple of months ago, we flew to Hawaii and drove up Mauna Kea. Next month, we'll climb Maine's 5,267-foot Katahdin, and the month after that we'll head west and hopefully summit 8,749-foot Guadalupe Peak (Texas), 12,633-foot Humphreys Peak (Arizona), and possibly 13,161-foot Wheeler Peak (New Mexico). This new game, highpointing, is a great excuse to travel around the country; one ascends the highest point of every state, and any method of ascent and descent is allowed. We've now run out of drive-ups; all we have left are the ones in which hiking's the only option. That's okay—the girls are physically ready for this year's adventures.

We still, of course, continue to hike the Whites.

Sage will probably finish the New Hampshire 4Ks in between this year's highpointing excursions, and Alex wants to complete the "winter 4Ks," hiking all forty-eight mountains strictly within winter seasons. She has a particular fondness for winter and wants to experience each of New Hampshire's highest peaks in the ice and snow.

Should either one decide to stop hiking tomorrow, that will be fine with me. I think I've made that abundantly clear, perhaps annoyingly so, to both my daughters. There's no pressure on either one of them to keep going. They've the rest of their lives to climb and explore. There's emphatically no expectation that we'll actually finish the highpointing list, since several of those mountains—Alaska's 20,320-foot Denali and Washington's 14,411-foot Rainier being two obvious examples—require extremely advanced mountaineering skills that my girls may or may not decide to procure. The decision to advance to that level will be theirs, and that decision is, at the very least, eight or nine years away. In the meantime, we'll have fun ascending the mountains Hugh and I feel the girls can handle.

Of course, if Alex and Sage get sick of all of this and stop hiking tomorrow, that's fine too. If they never want to set foot on a mountain again, that's also fine (but highly unlikely). They've both already fulfilled at least one incredible goal. Alex finished the New Hampshire forty-eight. Sage got up Tecumseh on her own two feet. Everything else is icing on their cakes. The primary missions have already been accomplished.

What matters now is that they know, from experience, that they can accomplish something big, something huge. What matters is that, for the rest of their lives, both my daughters understand that to reach a goal, they must put one foot in front of the other and persevere. They know that they must expect and prepare for challenges. They know to ignore the naysayers and, instead, to have faith in themselves and their abilities to learn what they need to know. Above all else, they know that little does not mean weak, that girls are indeed strong, and that practically anything is possible.

Whatever the future holds, I'm confident that Alex and Sage will continue to take strong steps forward, in whatever direction they choose.

Which will probably be up.

ACKNOWLEDGMENTS

Sage, my wonderful youngest daughter—you are every bit as strong and capable as your sister. Had I known you were eventually going to share Alex's love of hiking, I would have waited and written something that included your accomplishments as well as hers. Thank you for supporting Alex and this book. You've turned into quite the dynamo during the past twelve months and I've enjoyed our time together on the trails. You and your sister make a wonderful team; I look forward to watching the two of you fly higher and higher as you both grow older and more experienced. You are my beautiful bundle of sunshine, and I love you, kiddo.

Alex, this has been an amazing journey. Thanks for getting me out there. Thanks for asking me to write it all down. Thanks for being a kind and loving sister to Sage. Thanks for being all that you are. I love you.

Hugh, you stood back and allowed me to take our

very young daughters up the rugged New Hampshire mountains in all four seasons; you gave your blessing when I took the girls across remote regions of the United States for months during our 2010 highpointing spree; and now, as I write this in August 2011, you're in Massachusetts while the girls and I are en route to Texas so we can hike in an isolated region of the Chihuahuan Desert. Thank you for not blocking our way with unnecessary and overprotective barriers. We could not do what we do without your understanding and support. Thank you.

Rick Kipphut, thanks for your wonderful company and support throughout and beyond Alex's quest. Our family will always hold you and your lovely wife, Susan, near and dear to our hearts. Looking forward to many more hikes with you.

Dave Bear and LRiz, thanks for your support on Isolation and Owl's Head. Looking forward to spending more time with you on the trails.

Sandy Dimick, thanks for your hospitality, your friendship, and your ear. You, Troy, Kyle, and Kayla are wonderful people.

MWOBS and VFTT communities, thanks for the beta and conversations.

Thanks to the Appalachian Mountain Club for their creation of the New Hampshire Four Thousand Footer list and for their management of the White Mountain trails and hut system.

Mom and Dad, thanks, as always, for your support.

Thanks also, Mom, for being an early reader of what was then known as *Alex and the 4000-Foot Classroom.*

To Becky, Jim, Peter, Cathy, Steve, Laura, Emily, and David—thanks for being the source of much inspiration and encouragement.

A huge thank-you to Laurie Bernstein, my agent. Laurie, you've been a strong advocate of this book from the get-go. Many thanks for your unwavering enthusiasm. Thanks also to Rebecca Kaplan, Laurie's amazing assistant—I appreciate all your help!

To Sydny Miner at Crown—working with you is an absolute pleasure. Thanks for your editorial eye and enjoyable conversations.

To the rest of the team at Crown and Broadway Books, including Anna Thompson, Caroline Sill, Jonathan Lazzara, Catherine Pollock, Campbell Wharton, and Julie Cepler—many, many thanks for your guidance and support.

RESOURCES

The New Hampshire/White Mountains
Four Thousand Footers

WEBSITES

Ellozy, Mohamed. *Peakbagging the 4000 Footer Mountains of New England.* http://home.earthlink.net/~ellozy/index.html. Route descriptions, mileage, and elevation gain for each of the forty-eight Four Thousand Footers, plus additional information on various Vermont and Maine peaks.

The Four Thousand Footer Club. www.amc4000footer .org. The official website of the Four Thousand Footer Club. The official list of mountains, rules of the game, and annual ceremony information can be found here.

Metsky, David. *Hike the Whites!* http://hikethewhites .com. Helpful and interesting information about each of the forty-eight Four Thousand Footers.

BOOKS

Daniell, Gene, and Steven D. Smith. *AMC White Mountain Guide: Hiking Trails in the White Mountain National Forest*, 28th ed. Boston: Appalachian Mountain Club Books, 2007. Exhaustive list and detailed descriptions of all White Mountain trails.

Eng, Ronald C., ed. *Mountaineering: Freedom of the Hills: 50th Anniversary.* Seattle: Mountaineers Books, 2010. Comprehensive how-to guide for every aspect of climbing. Includes safety tips for situations of extreme weather and describes the "ten essentials."

Smith, Steven D., and Mike Dickerman. *The 4000-Footers of the White Mountains: A Guide and History,* 2nd ed. Littleton, NH: Bondcliff Books, 2008. Guide to ascending the Four Thousand Footers. Includes descriptions of the popular trails and helpful advice regarding winter climbs.

New Hampshire Hiking Forums

Hike New Hampshire. http://forum.hike-nh.com. Popular forum for New Hampshire hikers. Trip reports, general hiking-related topics, and such.

Mount Washington Observatory Forums. www .mountwashington.org/forums. Forums for those who enjoy Mount Washington. Both hiker and nonhiker members.

Rocks on Top. http://rocksontop.com. Forum for New Hampshire hikers.

Views from the Top. www.viewsfromthetop.com/ forums/index.php. Moderated forum catering to New England hikers. Trip reports, trail conditions, and general hiking-related conversation. Must be sponsored to join.

Mountain Weather Forecasts

National Oceanic and Atmospheric Administration (NOAA) Weather Forecasts. www.noaa.gov/wx.html. Comprehensive weather information for all parts of the United States.

White Mountains Observatory Higher Summits Forecast. www.mountwashington.org/weather/summit _forecast.php. Forecast for the White Mountain higher summits.

Kids and Nature Blogs

AMC's Great Kids, Great Outdoors. http://greatkids .outdoors.org. Tips on how to get children outside. Appalachian Mountain Club.

Children and Nature Network. www.childrenandnature .org. Network of researchers, parents, educators, and individuals committed to reconnecting children with nature.

Nature Rocks: Let's Go Explore. www.naturerocks.org. For families seeking nature-based activities.

overhead in the form of a huge eagle. It was known as the Mead of Poetry. 'There is not a single field of endeavour', it explained in *The Apple Star*, 'that is not furthered by beauty in one's words. But take care to add *exactly* the correct amount; a drop too much of this powerful brew can cause one to spout endless poetry, which could be disastrous!' Last of all Lulu added the crushed Velvet Flower, which was sacred to the Greek hunter-goddess Artemis and therefore meant to help females pursue their goals. And as Lulu mixed everything together, she imagined herself as the fleet-footed Artemis, chasing through the Olympian forests after wild beasts with her bow and arrow.

Lulu spread the thick paste out on some parchment and cut it into squares. Now came the chocolate. 'In its purest form, chocolate will stimulate mind, body and spirit,' Cassandra had said, reminding Lulu of what Mrs Pye had taught. Lulu melted the rare Madagascan chocolate very slowly, as instructed, then carefully poured the velvety, fragrant dark fluid over the squares.

Then came the moment Lulu always dreaded: what Ambrosia May called The Pang. The Pang came when you stopped concentrating on what you were doing (or, in Lulu's case, losing yourself in the stories) and noticed how desperately – how longingly! – you

'Hi A
Aileen
wet. W
making
away –
'Soak
sodden
'I'll pu
Aileen
'A cup of
'Yup,
joked Lulu
Lulu about
if she woul

But Aileen was
apparently unaware
thought Lulu; definit
eagerly back into
arranged the Chocol
she had lined with p
felt quite excited no
'Present,' said I
chocolates for Aileen
'You made these
she even seemed to
'Yeah!'
'That's great,
Lulu a hug and
have some.'
'Oh, not for me
'Nonsense!' sa
'You're never too
'No, really!' in
of a tummy ache
anyone else eith
for you.'
Aileen shrugge
'Wait!' said I
Aileen cast h
special...*wishing*

didn't sound too crazy. 'It's like snapping the wishbone, or finding the coin in the Christmas pud...you have to shut your eyes and make a wish each time you eat one.'

'I do, huh?'

'Yes, but think of a really *good* wish,' said Lulu. 'And, and...it's got to be the same wish you concentrate on every time...it's no good switching around or it won't work.'

'Oh-kay,' said Aileen slowly.

Now she really does think I'm nuts, thought Lulu. 'It's...a Pommy tradition, haven't you heard of it?' she added hastily. 'It's, uh,' – she stared at the basket, and a thought popped into her head – 'a Harvest Festival thing.'

'I thought Harvest Festival was over.'

'Well it is, but the wishing part's done later...when people are, y'know, thinking ahead to next year's crop.'

'Really?' said Aileen, a faintly amused look on her face. 'All right, this is bonkers, but what the heck!' She scrunched up her eyes and raised the chocolate to her mouth.

'Oh, one other thing!' said Lulu suddenly, her hand shooting out again to stop Aileen from eating the chocolate.

Aileen opened her eyes. 'What now?'

'Just...don't make it a love wish,' said Lulu. 'That won't work either.' This had been stated clearly in *The Apple Star* – there was a different section in the book for that sort of recipe – and it was an important thing for Aileen to know.

'Ha!' shrugged Aileen. 'Is that all?'

'Oh, and you've got fifteen choccies there, and you're to have three a day for five days.'

'Yes, doctor. Anything else?'

'Nope!' said Lulu at last. 'That's all.'

'OK!' said Aileen. 'All systems go, and...' She shut her eyes and popped the chocolate into her mouth.

'Blast off,' said Lulu.

Nuggets of Information

'Cooking again?' remarked Dad, popping his head around the kitchen door.

Lulu quickly hid *The Apple Star* behind her mixing bowl. 'Yeah, I just feel like it!' she said brightly. In fact, it was Sunday night, it was late, and she really didn't feel like it at all. But they had been out all day, and this was the only chance she would get to make her recipe for Zena and Chantrelle, which she needed for tomorrow.

The recipe was called Nuggets of Information. The Nuggets were cunningly disguised as the kind of junk food which, as Ambrosia May put it, 'no one who ever bothered to think about anything would eat'. They were designed simply to switch on the normally switched-off brain. 'As long as the brain is healthy, it is capable of intense thought and study,' said Ambrosia May.

Lulu had realised this was the perfect recipe for Zena and Chantrelle; she and Frenchy could serve it up at school lunch. They duly put themselves down as dinner monitors for the following week. Of course, making five days' supply for two people was no mean feat, but that was what Cassandra had advised. Thinking about Cassandra made Lulu feel anxious again; after Dad had gone she called her, but got the voicemail. This time, Lulu left Cassandra a message, asking her to call her. Then she rang Frenchy.

'Well, I know she was a bit agitated over that visitor,' agreed Frenchy. 'But it's not the first time she's been unreachable, is it? Remember when you wanted to make the Cupid Cakes, and you couldn't get hold of her for ages?'

'Yes, but then I had been out of touch for a while,' Lulu pointed out.

'I suppose so,' said Frenchy. 'But Lu, I do still think she's a bit flaky. I mean, *great*...but flaky. I'm sure it's nothing to worry about. You know, there could be something wrong with her phone; I'd write to her, if I were you.'

'Yeah,' said Lulu. 'I might do that.'

'By the way,' added Frenchy, 'how'd it go with the Chocolate Wishes; does Aileen seem any different yet?'

'I wouldn't know,' said Lulu. 'She's still spending loads of time in her room. Barely had a peep out of her.'

'Hey, maybe that's a good sign!' said Frenchy